CRIMINAL EVIDENCE

EIGHTH EDITION

STUDY GUIDE

John C.
KLOTTER

Professor Emeritus and Former Dean
School of Justice Administration
University of Louisville

Jefferson L.
INGRAM

University of Dayton

 LexisNexis™

 **anderson publishing**
A member of the LexisNexis Group

Criminal Evidence, Eighth Edition
STUDY GUIDE

Copyright © 2000, 2004
Anderson Publishing Co., a member of the LexisNexis Group

Phone 877-374-2919
Web Site www.lexisnexis.com/anderson/criminaljustice

This Study Guide was designed to be used in conjunction with *Criminal Evidence*, 8th ed. © 2004 by Anderson Publishing Co. (ISBN: 1-59345-558-4)

EDITOR Elisabeth Ebben • ACQUISITIONS EDITOR Michael C. Braswell

Contents

Introduction

This study guide has been prepared for students using *Criminal Evidence*, Eighth Edition, by John C. Klotter and Jefferson L. Ingram. The general purpose of the guide is to assist the student in learning the many evidence rules and concepts and, just as importantly, grasping the reasons for the rules and the rationale for the exceptions.

Description of the Course

This course provides a thorough study of the evidence rules, with specific emphasis on the application of these rules in preparing and presenting evidence. This includes a discussion of the history and approach to the study of evidence; proof by evidence and substitutes; general admissibility tests, including relevancy and materiality; opinion and expert testimony, and the hearsay rule; evidence by way of witness testimony, documents, scientific and real evidence; and exclusion of evidence on constitutional grounds. For a better understanding of the evidence rules, judicial decisions are cited and some are included in Part II of the book.

Objectives to be Accomplished in this Course

General—Every person involved in the criminal justice process must be familiar with the basic rules of evidence. For prosecution purposes, evidence has no value unless it is properly obtained, protected, prepared, and introduced at the trial of a person accused of a crime. Some evidence is admissible and some is not admissible, depending upon the rules established by the courts and legislatures. Evidence that is proper and has been determined to be legitimate should be prepared in such a way that it will not be excluded because of mishandling by a law enforcement officer or someone else in the criminal justice process.

Failure to thoroughly understand the rules of evidence not only affects the initial admissibility and weight of the evidence, but influences the case through all the steps in the criminal justice process. If a person guilty of crime is acquitted or is determined to be guilty of a lesser offense because of the inability or ineffectiveness of the person preparing and presenting the evidence, the criminal justice system breaks down. There can be no effective treatment of the person who is guilty of a crime if the case is not properly litigated. The parole officer or parole board cannot legitimately consider evidence that is made questionable by improper handling.

Those completing the course will not only have an understanding of the rules of evidence but also will be better able to understand the criminal justice process and the reasoning of courts and legislative bodies in establishing rules regarding the admissibility of evidence.

Specific performance objectives—The student who successfully completes this course will be able to:

1. Trace the historical development of the rules of evidence and explain the effect of that history on the rules finally adopted by the United States courts and legislative bodies.

2. Recognize that evidence rules are constantly evolving, that they are not infallible, and that they will be modified in the future.

3. State the rule relating to the burden of the prosecution in proving guilt and the rules concerning the burden of proof on the defense in a criminal case.

4. Describe the procedures used in introducing evidence, and the roles of the judge, jury, witnesses, and attorneys in presenting, challenging, and evaluation evidence.

5. Define *judicial notice*, distinguish between judicial notice of facts and judicial notice of law, and give some examples of each.

6. Explain what is meant by the term *substitute for evidence*. Give definitions of *presumption, stipulation,* and *inference.* Distinguish between presumptions of fact and presumptions of law, and give examples of the various types of substitutes for evidence.

7. Define *relevancy* and *materiality.* Give reasons for the exclusion of evidence even though it might be material and relevant and explain why some items are relevant and admissible and some are not.

8. Trace in detail the procedure to be followed in the examination and cross-examination of witnesses, and define such terms as *leading question, refreshing memory, past recollection recorded,* and *impeachment of witnesses.*

9. List the reasons for privileged communications, such as communications between husband and wife, between attorney and client, and between physician and patient. Summarize the scope of the privilege in each privileged communication situation.

10. Distinguish between expert testimony and non-expert, or lay testimony. Enumerate some of the subjects of expert and non-expert testimony and summarize the rules relating to cross-examination of expert witnesses.

11. Define *hearsay evidence* and the *hearsay rule* and give at least six exceptions to the hearsay rule with the requirements attached to each of these exceptions.

12. Define *documentary evidence*. Distinguish between documentary evidence, oral testimony, and real evidence, and explain specifically what is meant by *authentication* and *best evidence*.

13. List the requirements that must be met before real evidence is admitted into court, and summarize the rules concerning the introduction of such evidence as photographs, videotapes, X-rays, sound recordings, diagrams, and maps.

14. Explain the general rules relating to the results of examinations and tests, and specific rules that are peculiar to various types of tests, such as intoxication tests, blood-grouping tests, polygraph examinations, fingerprinting comparisons, ballistics experiments, speed detection readings, and forensic DNA test results.

15. Trace the development of the rules relating to the exclusion of evidence on constitutional grounds, such as illegally seized evidence, and evidence obtained in violation of the self-incrimination and due process provisions of the Constitution.

16. Brief cases, and sift from cases points of law relating to the introduction and exclusion of evidence.

17. Locate specific rules in the Federal Rules of Evidence for United States Courts and Magistrates, analyze these rules, and apply them to specific case situations.

Organization of the Material in the Study Guide

To make the material more usable by the student, each chapter includes objectives, a discussion outline, and review questions. Anticipating that the instructor will assign cases for the students to brief, the author has included some suggestions for briefing cases and a sample brief.

1. *Objectives of the Chapter*—To familiarize the students with the specific objectives of each chapter, these are stated in comprehensive terms.

2. *Discussion Outline*—Although the book itself is divided into sections and subsections, a discussion outline is included for each chapter. This should be used by the student to help in organizing notes and following the class discussion.

3. *Review Questions*—Review questions are included for each chapter. Some of these are general in nature and some are specific. Their purpose is to stimulate discussion and thinking and to help prepare the student for the examination.

Briefing Cases

In order to more thoroughly understand how to locate court cases, read cases for specific rules of law, and understand how court decisions determine criminal justice policies and procedures, cases may be assigned for briefing and for presentation to the class as a whole.

In reading cases, look for the point of law being considered and read the case thoroughly, not only for that point, but for the reasoning of the court in reaching its decision on that point. After the case has been thoroughly studied, it should be "briefed." The form of the brief is generally the form of the sample brief that follows.

State the essential **facts** of the case briefly, but in sufficient detail to give the factual situation on which the decision was made. The **issue** is the question the court is called upon to decide. This, too, should be brief but clear. The **decision** is the holding of the court, and the **reasoning** of the court is the rationale of the judges in reaching their conclusions.

The **rule of law** is a brief digest of what the court held. This is the rule that must be followed by lower courts and justice personnel, until changed by court decision, statute, or constitutional amendment. A section of the Constitution is *not* a rule of law, nor is a statute or code provision (see the rule in the sample brief).

Use the sample brief on the following pages as a guide.

Sample Brief

DICKERSON V. UNITED STATES
Supreme Court of the United States
530 U.S. 428 (2000)

Facts:

Dickerson was indicted for bank robbery, conspiracy to commit bank robbery, and using a firearm in the course of committing a crime of violence, all in violation of the applicable provisions of Title 18 of the United States Code. Subsequent to the decision in *Miranda v. Arizona*, Congress passed a law that purported to allow evidence to be admitted against defendants who had not received proper *Miranda* warnings. Before trial, Dickerson moved to suppress a statement he had made at an FBI field office, on the grounds that he had not received *Miranda* warnings before being interrogated. The district court heard his motion to suppress the evidence that was allegedly obtained in violation of the principles of *Miranda* and granted his motion to suppress. The United States attorney, on behalf of the federal government, took an interlocutory appeal to the United States Court of Appeals for the Fourth Circuit. The court of appeals reversed the district court even though it concluded that the *Miranda* warnings had been defectively given by federal agents. The court of appeals went on to conclude that Congress had the power to pass a statute reversing the Supreme Court's decision in *Miranda* and to allow a defendant's voluntary statements to be admissible in court against the defendant. The United States Supreme Court granted certiorari.

Issue:

Was the Supreme Court decision in *Miranda v. Arizona,* which mandated specific warnings to persons who are questioned while in custody, required by the Constitution?

Decision of the Court:

The Supreme Court decided that *Miranda*, being a constitutional decision of the Supreme Court, may not, in effect, be overruled by an Act of Congress and that a defendant who has not been properly warned may not have the statement used against him or her in court.

Reasoning of the Court:

The Supreme Court determined first determined that it was the clear intention of Congress to overrule the *Miranda v. Arizona* decision by instructing courts to consider only the totality of the circumstances regarding the voluntariness of a statement or confession in determining whether it should be admitted against a defendant.

The Supreme Court noted that it has supervisory authority over the federal courts to prescribe binding rules of evidence and procedure. It emphasized that while Congress has the ultimate authority to modify or set aside any such rules that are not constitutionally required or of constitutional dimension, Congress may not supersede the Court's decisions interpreting and applying the Constitution. The Court noted that it does not have a general supervisory role over state courts and could not have applied a rule as was devised in *Miranda v. Arizona* unless such a rule was of constitutional dimension and required by the Constitution of the United States.

The Court held that *Miranda* announced a constitutional rule that was demonstrated by the fact that both the *Miranda* case and two of its companion cases applied its rule to proceedings in state courts, and that the Court has consistently done so ever since.

The conclusion that *Miranda* was constitutionally based was also supported by the fact that that the *Miranda* case was replete with statements indicating that the majority thought it was announcing a constitutional rule.

Therefore, the warnings required under *Miranda v. Arizona* are constitutionally required and where their dictates are not met, the evidence must be excluded regardless of the intent of Congress to reverse the decision in *Miranda*.

The Supreme Court rejected arguments to overrule *Miranda v. Arizona*, noting that in cases of constitutional dimension, stare decisis weighs heavily against overruling *Miranda* at this time.

Citations to Support Judgment:
Carlisle v. United States, 517 U.S. 416 (1996).
Palermo v. United States, 360 U.S. 343 (1959).
City of Boerne v. Flores, 521 U.S. 507 (1997).
Stansbury v. California, 511 U.S. 318 (1994).

Rule of Law:
 Congress cannot reverse a decision of the Supreme Court where the result of a court case has been mandated by the Constitution of the United States. Where the Constitution requires that arrestees be properly warned prior to interrogation, and where the warnings are not properly given, the evidence must be excluded despite the clear intent of Congress to allow the evidence to be admissible in federal criminal trials.

Dissent:
 Justices Scalia and Thomas dissented. The dissenting judges felt that the decision was erroneous because *Miranda* was not originally a decision of constitutional dimensions. The two justices noted that to those who understand the judicial process, it will be obvious that the *Dickerson* decision was not merely a reaffirmation of *Miranda*, but a radical revision of the most significant element of *Miranda* and gives the *Miranda* rationale a permanent place in our jurisprudence that will not likely ever be overruled.

Chapter 1

History and Development
of Rules of Evidence

Objectives

The rules of evidence have developed over many years. To fully understand the influence of history on the present-day rules, that history must be studied and interpreted because much of the present practice of the rules of evidence has evolved through the experience of prior generations. The first objective of this chapter is to help the student appreciate the empirical experience that has gone into the development of the rules of evidence under English law and the development of those rules in the United States. The second objective is to prepare the student to recognize that the rules today are not inflexibly static, but may be changed by present and future generations to satisfy the evolving needs of society.

The objectives of this chapter are to:

1. Develop an understanding of the procedures followed by the various tribunals in other civilizations and periods in determining guilt or innocence.

2. Trace the development of the English jury system, which has greatly influenced the complex evidence rules developed in that country and the United States.

3. Trace the development of the rules of evidence in the United States and explain how these rules are modified by court decisions and legislative bodies.

4. Make the student aware that the rules of evidence in state and federal courts continually change in subtle as well as obvious ways, and that they will continue to evolve as new situations arise. The student should become aware of the factors that influence the direction of changes in the rules of evidence

Discussion Outline

§1.1   Introduction

§1.2   Early Attempts to Determine Guilt or Innocence
     A. Egyptian Legal System
     B. Mesopotamian Legal System
     C. Hebrew Legal System
     D. Chinese Legal System
     E. Greek Legal System
     F. Roman Legal System

§1.3   Modern Legal Systems—Romanesque System
     A. Development of the System
     B. Countries Following this System

§1.4   Anglican System
     A. Development of the System in England
     B. The Influence of the Norman Conquest
     C. Development of the Jury System
     D. Countries Following this System

§1.5   Development of the Rules of Evidence in the United States
     A. Constitutional Provisions
     B. As Determined by the Courts
     C. As Determined by Congressional or Legislative Enactment
     D. Adoption of the Federal Rules of Evidence
     E. Preparation of the Uniform Rules of Evidence

§1.6   Application of the Rules of Evidence in State and Federal Courts
     A. How Rules Are Established for State Courts
     B. How Rules Are Established for Federal Courts
     C. Federal Rules of Evidence and the Uniform Rules Have Not Created Uniformity

§1.7   Future Development of the Rules of Evidence
     A. New Rules and Interpretations Will Reflect Changed Circumstances
     B. Old Rules Give Way to Modern Interpretations and Needs

§1.8   Summary

Review Questions

1. Why is it necessary or even desirable to review the practices followed by courts in other civilizations and earlier periods of history in determining the guilt or innocence of persons accused of crimes? (§1.2)

2. In what way did the early Hebrew legal system differ from the Chinese legal system? (§1.2)

3. The Greek legal system influenced the Roman legal system, and that in turn influenced modern rules of evidence. Trace this development. (§1.2)

4. According to Wigmore, three primary world systems exist today. What are they? (§1.3)

5. How does the Romanesque legal system differ from the English, or Anglican, system? (§§1.3, 1.4)

6. Trace the development of the jury system. What are the advantages and disadvantages of the jury system? (§1.4)

7. How are the rules of evidence determined in the United States and what process is used to change the rules? (§1.5)

8. Define the process followed in preparing and adopting the Federal Rules of Evidence for the United States Courts and Magistrates. How has the adoption of these rules affected the admissibility of evidence in federal and state courts? (§1.5)

9. What effect do the decisions of the United States Supreme Court have on state rules of evidence? (§1.6)

10. Should the rules of evidence be changed as society changes? Who should have the responsibility for modifying or rewriting the rules? (§1.7)

11. In your opinion, are the rules of evidence in the United States overly restrictive? Discuss. (§1.7)

12. In *Trammel v. United States*, the Supreme Court altered the privilege that a defendant spouse could prevent a witness spouse from testifying against the other. What was the rationale of the Court in making a change in the interpretation of established law? (§1.7)

13. In *Funk v. United States*, the United States Supreme Court reviewed the law relating to the competency of a wife to testify on behalf of her husband in a criminal case. What was the opinion of the justices in that case concerning the modification of the traditional rule? What was the decision of the court concerning the basis of the rules and the modification of the rules?

Chapter 2
Approach to the Study
of Criminal Evidence

Objectives

Evidence rules, as established by courts and legislative bodies, are difficult to understand. There is less misunderstanding, however, if the reasons for those rules are explained to those who are studying them. Also, if the student understands how the witness who presents the evidence fits into the overall trial procedure, there will be more incentive for learning and understanding the rules. The objective of this chapter is to develop a general understanding of the reasons for the rules and procedures established to protect the person accused of a crime.

The objectives of this chapter are to:

1. Define the essential words and phrases that must be understood to enable the student to comprehend the material presented.

2. Understand the different types and categories of evidence and be able to give an example of each.

3. Explain why the rules of evidence are necessary to allow the orderly progress of a fair criminal trial.

4. Develop an understanding of the evolution of the rules of evidence made necessary by the jury system and the reasons these rules are applied in criminal cases.

5. State and explain the five general reasons for excluding otherwise pertinent evidence.

6. Distinguish between the rules as they are applied in criminal and civil cases and emphasize the greater degree of proof necessary in criminal prosecutions.

7. State in specific terms the route that evidence takes from the time it is discovered until the time it is introduced in court and to comprehend how the representatives in the criminal justice system use evidence.

8. Introduce the procedures followed in offering evidence in court and for challenging evidence that may be excludable under the rules of evidence.

9. Explain how appellate courts, judges at probation hearings, and parole boards consider and evaluate evidence following criminal trials.

Discussion Outline

§2.1   Introduction

§2.2   Definitions
    A. Evidence
    B. Legal Evidence
    C. Direct Evidence
    D. Circumstantial Evidence
    E. Testimony
    F. Documentary Evidence
    G. Real Evidence
    H. Prima Facie Evidence
    I. Proof
    J. Cumulative Evidence
    K. Corroborative Evidence
    L. Relevant Evidence
    M. Material Evidence
    N. Competent Evidence
    O. Hearsay Evidence

§2.3   Reasons for the Rules of Evidence

§2.4   Reasons for Excluding Evidence
    A. Protect Interests and Relationships
    B. Avoid Undue Prejudice to the Accused
    C. Prohibit Consideration of Unreliable Evidence
    D. Reduce Violations of Constitutional Safeguards
    E. Conserve Time

§2.5   Rules of Evidence in Criminal Cases Compared to Rules of Evidence in Civil Cases
    A. Burden of Proof
    B. Jury Verdict
    C. Weight of Evidence

§2.6   Pretrial Flow of Evidence
    A. Police
    B. Prosecutor
    C. Magistrate
    D. Grand jury
    E. Criminal Court—Arraignment
    F. Criminal Court—Pretrial Hearing

Review Questions

1. Explain the difference between direct evidence and circumstantial evidence. (§2.2)

2. Distinguish *testimony, documentary evidence,* and *real evidence.* (§2.2)

3. What is the difference between evidence and proof? (§2.2)

4. Why have courts and legislatures developed such complex rules of evidence in the United States? (§2.3)

5. In discussing the rationale for excluding evidence in some situations, five explanations were listed. List and give an example of each. (§2.4)

6. State at least three ways in which the approach to the use of evidence in civil cases differs from the approach in criminal cases. (§2.5)

7. Must all serious criminal prosecutions be initiated by a presentation of evidence to a grand jury in state criminal cases? (§2.6)

8. Trace the flow of evidence from the time it is discovered until it is presented in court. (§2.6)

9. What is the role of the prosecutor in handling evidence at trial? The role of the judge? The role of the jury? (§2.7)

10. How is evidence that was collected in the early stages of the justice process used at probation hearings and when considering parole? (§§2.9, 2.10)

11. In *State v. Perkins*, the defendant claimed that his case was prejudiced by the judge asking questions on cross-examination. What was the opinion of the reviewing court relating to the roles of the judge, the jurors, and the prosecutor in this criminal case? (*State v. Perkins*, Part II).

Chapter 3
Burden of Proof

Objectives

In a criminal case, the investigator and prosecutor must compile and present sufficient evidence to convince the jury or the judge that the accused is guilty beyond a reasonable doubt. This burden of proof rests on the prosecution. Although a defendant does not generally have a burden of proof, this chapter discusses the burden that an accused might have in rebutting prosecution evidence in order to avoid a conviction. In cases involving affirmative defenses, the defense may have a burden of proof limited to establishing the affirmative defense by a preponderance of the evidence or, in some cases, by clear and convincing evidence. The objective of this chapter is first to define burden of proof; second, to disclose the important role of those involved in the criminal justice system in regard to establishing proof; and third, to discuss some of the specific areas where the burden of proof is particularly important in criminal cases.

The objectives of this chapter are to:

1. Distinguish burden of proof in a civil case and burden of proof in a criminal case.

2. Define the terms *burden of proof, burden of going forward,* and *burden of persuasion.*

3. Distinguish *preponderance of the evidence, clear and convincing evidence,* and *beyond a reasonable doubt.*

4. Understand that the burden of proof can be allocated to the defendant with respect to proving affirmative defenses.

5. State the rationale and explain the theory that requires the prosecution to prove all elements of a crime beyond a reasonable doubt in order to meet due process requirements.

6. Examine and explain the general rules relating to the burden placed upon the defendant in a criminal case.

7. Emphasize the decisions of the Supreme Court that hold that the defendant cannot be required to prove his innocence.

8. Define "affirmative defenses" and state the rules necessary to establish the existence of such defenses.

9. Discuss the legal burdens on the prosecution and defense when the defendant raises the affirmative defense of alibi.

10. Explain the burden of proof necessary to prevail when asserting the affirmative defense of insanity.

11. Distinguish between the two different rules regarding the degree of evidence required to rebut the presumption of sanity.

12. Understand the burden of proof that may be placed upon a defendant by the state concerning the affirmative defense of self-defense and that some jurisdictions merely require that the defendant raise the defense and present some evidence.

13. State the law regarding the presumption of the sufficiency of the evidence once a defendant has been convicted.

Discussion Outline

§3.1   Introduction

§3.2   Definitions and Distinctions
         A. Burden of Proof
         B. Burden of Going Forward
         C. Burden of Persuasion

§3.3   Preponderance of the Evidence

§3.4   Clear and convincing Evidence

§3.5   Beyond a Reasonable Doubt
         A. Definition of Reasonable Doubt
         B. Reasons for the Reasonable Doubt Requirement
         C. Instructions on Reasonable Doubt

§3.6   Burden on the Prosecution
         A. Burden to Show that a Crime Has Been Perpetrated (*CorpusDelicti*)
         B. Burden to Show Criminal Responsibility

§3.7   Burden to Prove All Elements of the Crime

§3.8   Burden on the Accused

Review Questions

1. What is meant by the statement "The burden of proof of guilt in a criminal case is on the prosecution throughout the trial"? (§3.1)

2. Define burden of proof, burden of going forward, and burden of persuasion. (§3.2)

3. Explain why the *burden of going forward with the evidence* may shift from the prosecution to the defense and may even shift back to the prosecution. (§3.2)

4. What is the difference between *preponderance of the evidence* and *beyond a reasonable doubt*? Define *beyond a reasonable doubt*. (§§3.3, 3.5)

5. Is there a difference between *clear and convincing evidence* and *a preponderance of the evidence*? If so, what is the difference? (§§3.3, 3.4)

6. What type of cases may use the legal standard of clear and convincing evidence and preponderance of the evidence? (§§3.3, 3.4)

7. If the trial judge fails to instruct the jury about an essential element of the crime and that the jury must find that element beyond a reasonable doubt, must the conviction be reversed? Explain. (§3.5)

8. What is the rationale for requiring the standard of beyond a reasonable doubt in a criminal case, and not requiring this in a civil case? (§3.6)

9. Why did the Supreme Court of the United States hold that proof beyond a reasonable doubt in a criminal case is a constitutional requirement? (§3.5)

10. The rule is that the burden of proving guilt does not shift from the prosecution in a criminal case. Does this mean that the accused is not responsible for proving any claim? Explain. (§3.6)

11. In order to convict a person of the crime charged, each of the elements of the crime must be proved. For example, in a murder case, the elements are: (1) there was an intentional killing of (2) one person by another person, (3) with malice aforethought. What is the result if the prosecution fails to prove any of the elements beyond a reasonable doubt? (§3.7)

12. If, in an assault and battery case, the accused claims that he or she was not near the place where the alleged incident took place, does the accused have the responsibility to prove that he or she was not at the scene? What degree of evidence is required? (§3.10)

13. If *specific intent* is an element of a crime, is it error for the judge to instruct the jury that "it is reasonable to infer that a person intends the natural and probable consequences of an act knowingly done?" Explain. (§3.8)

14. In some instances the defendant has the burden of proving affirmative defenses. Does this violate due process? (§3.9)

15. If a defendant makes a threshold showing of proof for an affirmative defense, should the judge offer a jury instruction covering that affirmative defense? (§§3.8, 3.9)

16. In some jurisdictions, courts have held that the issue of alibi is an affirmative defense, and when asserted, the burden of proof by a preponderance of the evidence rests with the defendant. What is meant by an alibi defense? Why do some states require that the defense give notice in advance to the prosecution that alibi witnesses are to be used at the trial? (§3.10)

17. If the defendant introduces evidence of insanity, must the prosecution prove sanity beyond a reasonable doubt? Discuss the various rules. (§3.11)

18. If the defendant in a criminal case pleads self-defense, what burden rests with the defense? (§3.12)

19. After the triers of fact render a guilty verdict, may the reviewing court set aside a conviction if it finds that no rational trier of fact could logically have found the defendant guilty beyond a reasonable doubt? Explain your answer. (§3.13)

20. What is the effect of the beyond a reasonable doubt requirement on the responsibility of the law enforcement investigator? (§3.14)

21. In the case of *Victor v. Nebraska*, the United States Supreme Court considered the constitutionality of attempts to define "reasonable doubt." What was the decision of the Court concerning: (1) the requirement of a reasonable doubt instruction; (2) the wording of an instruction; and (3) the correctness of the instructions in the cases. (*Victor v. Nebraska*, Part II)

22. In the case of *Martin v. Ohio*, the defendant was tried in state court for aggravated murder. What was the decision of the United States Supreme Court concerning the Ohio practice of placing on the defendant the burden of proving that she was acting in self-defense when she allegedly committed the murder? Do other states follow the same rule regarding the burden of proof when self-defense is claimed by the defendant? (*Martin v. Ohio*, Part II)

23. In the case of *People v. Gordon,* the defendant was convicted of possession of a stolen motor vehicle. Among other things, the defendant claimed on appeal that the state's evidence failed to prove the essential elements of the offense. What was the opinion of the reviewing court concerning the burden of proving each element of the crime, the presumption of innocence, and the result if the state fails to prove one element? What was the conclusion of the reviewing court? (*People v. Gordon*, Part II)

Chapter 4
Proof via Evidence

Objectives

To appreciate the importance of evidence, one must understand the procedures followed in presenting evidence in court and the many approaches available to the parties for challenging evidence, especially during the pretrial phase. Also, the student of criminal evidence will feel more comfortable about the process if he or she understands the roles that the judge, attorneys, and witnesses play in preparing and introducing evidence. It is crucial that the student develop an understanding of the role of the jury in evaluating the evidence. The first objective of this chapter is to explain the procedure for presenting evidence and define the roles of the judge, jury, and witnesses.

A secondary objective of this chapter is to explain that direct and circumstantial evidence possess theoretically equal force, weight, and believability, and that proof of a fact may be made with either direct or circumstantial evidence, or both.

The objectives of this chapter are to:

1. Develop an understanding of the purpose and importance of pretrial motions relating to the admissibility of evidence.

2. Comprehend the difference between an objection based on the form of the question and an objection based upon the substance of the question.

3. Develop an understanding of the order followed in presenting the state's evidence and the defendant's evidence in a criminal case, as well as the rationale for the order of presentation of evidence.

4. Summarize the procedure for offering and challenging evidence by the use of specific objections that preserve the record for appellate purposes.

5. With respect to the admission or exclusion of evidence, enumerate at least five responsibilities of the trial judge in a criminal case.

6. Clearly describe the function of the jury in a criminal case, including its duties and limitations.

7. Emphasize the role of the witness—especially in a criminal case—in preparing and making evidence available to the trier of fact.

8. Indicate the responsibilities of the prosecuting attorney and defense attorney before and during the trial in a criminal case.

9. Define direct and circumstantial evidence and understand that, although both have equal weight, juries may give diminished weight to circumstantial evidence.

Discussion Outline

§4.1   Introduction

§4.2   Pretrial Motions Pertaining to Evidence

§4.3   General Approach to Admissibility
        A. Objections as to Form
        B. Objections as to Substance

§4.4   Order of Presenting Evidence at the Trial
        A. State's Case-in-Chief
        B. Defense's Case-in-Chief
        C. State's Case in Rebuttal
        D. Defense's Case in Rejoinder

§4.5   Procedure for Offering and Challenging Evidence

§4.6   Role of the Trial Judge in Evidence Matters
        A. Determines Before Trial Whether Evidence Is Admissible at the Trial
        B. Acts on Motions Regarding Evidence During the Trial
        C. Makes Decisions Concerning the Constitutionality of Law Enforcement Activities
        D. Protects Witnesses from Overzealous Examination and Cross-Examination by Counsel
        E. Takes Judicial Notice
        F. Determines Competency of the Witness to Testify
        G. Rules on Issues of Law
        H. Acts as Finder of Fact in Some Cases

§4.7   Function of the Jury
        A. Hears and Evaluates Evidence
        B. Determines Weight to Give Testimony
        C. Renders Decisions Based on Evidence

§4.8   Role of Witnesses
        A. Introduces Evidence
        B. Offers Testimony
        C. Compulsory Process Can Require Attendance
        D. Defense Has Constitutional Right to Cross-Examine

§4.9   Prosecuting Attorney's Responsibilities
    A. Prepares the State's Case for Trial
    B. Evaluates the Evidence and Determines Whether the Case Should Be Prosecuted
    C. Guides the Prosecution's Case During the Trial
    D. Examines the State's Witnesses and Cross-Examines the Defendant's Witnesses
    E. Makes Opening and Closing Statements
    F. In Some Cases Consults with the Defendant's Attorney Before Entering Into a Plea Agreement
    G. Has the Duty to Furnish the Defendant with Exculpatory Evidence in the Possession of the Prosecution

§4.10 Defense Attorney's Responsibilities
    A. Interviews the Defense Witnesses
    B. Reviews the State's Evidence and Evidence for the Defendant
    C. Prepares the Defendant's Case for Trial
    D. Cross-Examines Witnesses for the Prosecution and Examines Defense Witnesses
    E. Makes Opening and Closing Statements for the Defense
    F. In Some Cases Works with the Prosecution in Negotiating a Plea

§4.11 Admissibility and Weight of Direct and Circumstantial Evidence
    A. Direct Evidence
    B. Circumstantial Evidence

§4.12 Summary

Review Questions

1. The jury, and in some instances the judge, must make decisions regarding guilt or innocence in a criminal case. What sources of information do the fact finders use to make these decisions? (§4.1)

2. Prior to a criminal trial, the prosecuting and defense attorneys have an opportunity to make pretrial motions. Name at least three subjects of pretrial motions. (§4.2)

3. When a witness on the stand is questioned by the attorneys or judge, the opposing attorney may challenge or object to the questions asked. Under what conditions may the objection be made as to form? As to substance? (§4.3)

4. The courts have established procedures for presenting evidence in court. In the usual criminal case, what is the order of presenting the evidence? What are the limitations of each party in offering rebuttal evidence and rejoinder evidence? (§4.4)

5. Why does the prosecution present its evidence before the defense presents its evidence? (§4.4)

6. If the introduction of evidence is challenged by the opposing party, what is the procedure for offering the objection and for preparing the record to allow for an appeal of a judge's adverse ruling? (§4.5)

7. Why must an attorney's objection to the introduction of evidence be made in a timely manner? (§4.5)

8. The judge, jury, witnesses, and attorneys play important parts in evidentiary matters. Name at least five responsibilities of the trial judge in relation to the introduction of evidence. Under what circumstances may a judge make comments to the jury? (§4.6)

9. What factors are used to determine the propriety of any comment by the trial judge in a jury trial? (§4.6)

10. What limitations does a judge have when making comments on the evidence? (§4.6)

11. What is the function of the jury in a criminal case? (§4.7)

12. What limitations should a jury or a juror observe when sitting or deliberating on a case? (§4.7)

13. What is the role of the witness—especially a law enforcement witness—in a criminal case? (§4.8)

14. In 1985, the Supreme Court of the United States, in a very comprehensive opinion, discussed the responsibilities of the prosecutor and the defense counsel. What was the standard of conduct that was established by the Supreme Court for prosecutors? Does the standard of conduct for the prosecution differ from that for the defense? (§4.9)

15. What are the responsibilities of the prosecutor in a criminal case? (§4.9)

16. What are the responsibilities of the defense attorney in a criminal case? (§4.9)

17. Why must a prosecutor give the defense significant evidence prior to trial if the defense asks to see exculpatory prosecution evidence? (§4.9)

18. In preparing and prosecuting a criminal case, what discretion do prosecutors generally have? (§4.9)

19. What are the responsibilities of the defense counsel in a criminal case? (§4.10)

20. In the case of *Nix v. Whiteside,* the Supreme Court considered the role of the defense attorney when the defendant indicates to his attorney that the defendant plans to commit perjury. What was the opinion of the Court? (§4.10)

21. Explain the difference between direct evidence and circumstantial evidence. (§4.11)

22. As a practical matter, is there a difference between the weight given by a jury to direct evidence and circumstantial evidence? Should there be any difference? (§4.11)

23. Is evidence that is characterized as "circumstantial" admissible at trial in a criminal case? If admissible, is circumstantial evidence less persuasive than direct evidence? Explain. (§4.11)

24. The *Brady* doctrine states that it is reversible error for the prosecutor to use evidence that he or she knows or should know is untrue and to withhold exculpatory evidence favorable to the defense. In the case of *Maddox v. Montgomery*, the Court of Appeals for the Eighth Circuit enumerated four types of situations in which the *Brady* doctrine applies. What are these four situations? (*Maddox v. Montgomery*, Part II, and §4.9)

Chapter 5
Judicial Notice

Objectives

Although the prosecution and the defense generally have the burden of establishing facts by producing sworn witnesses, authenticated documents, or real evidence, in order to save time, the jury or other fact finder may also consider substitutes for evidence. As a substitute for evidence, judicial notice takes the place of evidence, possessing equal force and effect. The effect as a substitute for evidence is so strong that once a fact has been judicially noticed, the court will not permit evidence that contradicts the judicially noticed fact. The purpose of this chapter is to define the terms *judicial notice of facts* and *judicial notice of law*, to explain the judicial notice process, and to caution against relying too heavily on judicial notice as a substitute for evidence.

The objectives of this chapter are to:

1. Introduce the reader to the "substitutes for evidence" rationale and to define and distinguish substitutes for evidence (judicial notice, presumptions, inferences, and stipulations).

2. Define judicial notice and list the two prerequisites for taking judicial notice.

3. Understand that the Federal Rules of Evidence cover only "adjudicative facts" that concern the dispute between the parties that may be determinative of the outcome of the case.

4. Enable the student to understand the reasoning of courts and legislatures in establishing rules concerning what facts *must* be judicially noticed and what facts *may* be judicially noticed.

5. Enable the student to comprehend that appellate courts may generally take judicial notice of facts that would have been appropriate for a trial court to have judicially noticed.

6. Develop the understanding that judicial notice does not refer to and is not limited to the personal knowledge of the presiding trial judge.

7. Enumerate the traditional kinds of facts that may be judicially noticed and explain the limitations applied in each category as developed by the courts and legislatures. Historical facts, geographical facts, scientific facts, dictionary definitions, etc., are considered.

8. To enhance the understanding that judicial notice in one jurisdiction will not necessarily cover the exact facts that would be properly noticed in a different jurisdiction.

9. Increase the student's knowledge of the rules relating to judicial notice of laws and the special requirements and limitations that center on the use of this type of judicial notice. Included is a consideration of the rules concerning judicial notice of federal laws, laws of other states, laws of foreign countries, municipal ordinances, and administrative regulations.

10. Trace the judicial notice process, beginning with the motion that judicial notice be taken and concluding with the stage at which facts are judicially noticed by the judge.

11. Understand that a judge may take judicial notice even when no request to do so has been made by either the prosecution or the defense.

12. To enhance awareness that an attorney's reliance on judicial notice carries dangers when a judge refuses to take notice and the party does not have evidence to present that will cover the facts that were refused judicial notice.

13. Using case situations, apply judicial notice concepts in criminal cases.

Discussion Outline

Review Questions

1. When the burden of proof has been properly allocated, and the prosecution has the burden of proving the case, why should a court take judicial notice of adjudicative facts without the necessity of introducing evidence to actually prove the facts? (§5.1)

2. Define the term *judicial notice* and give some examples. (§5.2)

3. There are two categories of judicial notice: *judicial notice of facts* and *judicial notice of laws*. What are the limits placed upon the kinds of facts that may be judicially noticed? (§5.3)

4. Why is predicting what facts a court will judicially notice difficult to accomplish with precision? (§5.3)

5. Generally, a court may take judicial notice of matters of general knowledge within the jurisdiction. In such instances, is it necessary that the matter be familiar to the majority of mankind? To the judge? Explain. (§5.4)

6. What are some examples of situations in which a court has taken judicial notice of historical facts? Is the judge required to take judicial notice of historical facts? Explain. (§5.5)

7. May a trial court take judicial notice of the fact that Chicago is approximately 790 miles from New York? Would the same reasoning apply if the trial court took judicial notice of the exact length of time it takes to travel from Chicago to New York? (§5.6)

8. Are there any cases that approve taking judicial notice of the scientific validity of blood-grouping tests? DNA test results? Discuss. Give other examples of judicial notice of scientific facts. What is the test for admission of novel scientific evidence? (§5.7)

9. How should a judge determine that a scientific principle has reached the level of general acceptability to the scientific community so that it is no longer subject to scientific dispute and, thus, is an appropriate topic for judicial notice? (§5.7)

10. May a court take judicial notice of the meaning of certain words or symbols? Give some examples. (§5.8)

11. What is the rationale for authorizing a trial court to take judicial notice of certain laws? (§5.9)

12. What are some examples of situations in which a court may take judicial notice of laws? (§5.10)

13. Must a court take judicial notice of the laws of the United States and of the state in which it sits? (§§5.10, 5.11)

14. Under what conditions may judicial notice be taken of municipal ordinances? (§5.14)

15. Give some examples of situations in which a court takes judicial notice of administrative regulations. (§5.15)

16. What process is followed in taking judicial notice and making the fact finder aware of the decision? (§5.17)

17. If judicial notice should be taken for well-known and undisputable facts, why might it be important to supply the judge with the necessary information that would otherwise prove the facts? (§5.17)

18. Are courts more reluctant to permit the use of judicial notice in criminal cases as compared to civil cases? Give reasons for your answer. (§5.18)

19. In the case of *State v. Vejvoda,* the defendant was convicted in county court of drunk driving and he appealed. One of his grounds for appeal was the claim that the court improperly took judicial notice of facts establishing the site of the events on which his conviction was based. While the judge took judicial notice of the fact that the accident occurred at the corner of two streets, there was no evidence that these streets were in the county where the defendant was tried. What was the

opinion of the Supreme Court of Nebraska concerning the validity of the trial judge taking judicial notice or failing to take judicial notice of facts? What did the court say concerning the personal knowledge of a judge in reference to taking judicial notice of a fact? (*State v. Vejvoda*, Part II)

20. In the case of *Fawcett v. State*, the defendant was convicted of forgery, criminal impersonation, and shoplifting. He appealed the conviction, arguing, among other things, that the court erred in improperly taking judicial notice of Fawcett's identity. What was the decision of the reviewing court in regard to the scope of judicial notice? May the court take judicial notice of a fact if there is a possibility of dispute of that fact? Is it appropriate to take judicial notice to establish a defendant's identity? (*Fawcett v. State*, Part II).

21. In the case of *Louisiana v. Richardson*, the trial court had been asked to take judicial notice of jurisdiction and venue in a case in which the defendant was convicted of distribution of a Schedule II controlled dangerous substance, cocaine. The prosecution argued that the trial court could properly take judicial notice that a recognizable location was inside a parish even though the parish was never specifically mentioned by name. What was the decision of the reviewing court in regard to the taking of judicial notice concerning jurisdiction and venue? (*Louisiana v. Richardson*, Part II).

22. In the case of *Robinson v. Georgia*, the trial court convicted the defendant at a bench trial of driving under the influence of alcohol. He appealed his conviction. One of his allegations was that the trial court improperly took judicial notice of venue. Why was this decision of the reviewing court different from the decision in *Louisiana v. Richardson*? Do some states follow different rules with respect to venue and judicial notice? Explain. (*Robinson v. Georgia*, Part II).

Chapter 6
Presumptions, Inferences, and Stipulations

Objectives

In addition to evaluating the usual types of evidence introduced through testimony and the introduction of physical objects and exhibits, in making decisions in criminal cases, juries may consider information that is available by way of presumptions, inferences, and stipulations. These legal devices serve as substitutes for evidence because testimony and physical evidence are not actually introduced. The purpose of this chapter is not only to define the terms and to develop an understanding of these concepts but also to explain when the attorney may appropriately rely upon presumptions, inferences, and stipulations, and when reliance on substitutes for evidence would not be proper. This chapter offers some examples of presumptions, inferences, and stipulations in the context of criminal prosecutions that assist in determining when their use should prove helpful in the presentation of a case by a particular party.

The objectives of this chapter are to:

1. Define and distinguish the evidentiary concepts of *presumption, inference,* and *stipulation.*

2. State in specific terms three reasons for allowing presumptions, inferences, and stipulations as substitutes for evidence.

3. Distinguish between presumptions of law and presumptions of fact and give examples of each.

4. Understand the logical reasoning and constitutional considerations that support the development and continued existence of presumptions as a substitute for evidence.

5. Understand that presumptions have the same evidentiary weight as if evidence had been actually introduced.

6. Emphasize the significance of the presumption of innocence in a criminal case and, by using case situations, clarify the requirements regarding instructions to the jury relating to the presumption of innocence.

7. Develop an understanding that most presumptions are rebuttable with proper evidence and understand why conclusive presumptions are unconstitutional in criminal cases.

8. List situations in which the presumption rules are most often considered in criminal cases. Among these are the presumption of sanity, the presumption against suicide, and the presumption that a person intends the ordinary consequences of his or her voluntary acts.

9. Distinguish between true presumptions and inferences.

10. Understand and be able to explain the legal test set forth by the Supreme Court to determine whether a particular presumption passes the test for constitutionality.

11. Make clear the consequences of the presumption that "all persons are presumed to have knowledge of the law."

12. Referring to cases, explain the limits on legislative bodies and lower courts in utilizing the presumption as a substitute for evidence.

13. Define *stipulation* and distinguish stipulations from other evidence substitutes.

14. Understand why a party would want to agree to a stipulation with the opposing party and why strategy might dictate a refusal to stipulate to particular facts.

15. Give examples of situations in which stipulations are important in the criminal justice process.

Discussion Outline

§6.1   Introduction

§6.2   Definitions and Distinctions
       A. Presumptions
       B. Inferences
       C. Stipulations

§6.3   Reasons for Presumptions and Inferences
       A. Procedural Technique
       B. Public Policy
       C. Allowance of Normal Governmental Activities

§6.4   Presumptions of Law

Review Questions

1. What is the difference between a presumption and an inference? Between a presumption and a stipulation? (§6.2)

2. How does the use of a presumption affect the burden of going forward with the evidence? (§6.2)

3. Explain how proof of a basic fact involved in a presumption gives rise to the belief that a second fact, the presumed fact, actually exists or is true. (§6.2)

4. What real and potential benefits accrue to the court and to the contending parties by virtue of using presumptions and inferences in criminal trials? (§6.3)

5. Define a presumption of law and give at least two examples of such a presumption. (§6.4)

6. What is the difference between a presumption of law and a presumption of fact? (§§6.4, 6.5)

7. There are four classes of presumptions discussed in your text. Name, define, and give one example of each. (§6.6)

8. In a criminal case, the defendant is rebuttably presumed to be innocent. Is it necessary for the judge to give an instruction on the presumption of innocence? Elaborate. Does the presumption of innocence prevail on appeal, after conviction? (§6.8)

9. Because every defendant is presumed innocent until proven guilty, does a trial judge have to give a jury instruction explaining this presumption? Explain. (§6.8)

10. There is a rule of evidence that states that every person is presumed to be sane. What is the legal effect of this presumption? Is this presumption rebuttable or conclusive? Explain. (§6.9)

11. According to the provisions of the 1984 Comprehensive Crime Control Act, mental disease or defect does not constitute a defense in federal court unless, at the time of commission of the act, and as a result of severe mental disease or defect, the defendant was unable to appreciate the nature and quality of the wrongfulness of the acts. Under this provision, who has the burden of proving the defense of insanity? What degree of proof is required? (§6.9)

12. If a state places the burden of proving insanity on a defendant, because the state may presume all persons are sane, why does this not result in a defendant having to unconstitutionally disprove an element of the crime charged? (§6.9)

13. What is the rationale for the presumption against suicide? (§6.10)

14. Some states still apply the rule that proof of the accused's knowing possession of recently stolen goods gives rise to the presumed fact that the defendant was the thief. Discuss the conditions that must be met if this presumption is applied. (§6.11)

15. Some courts have given the instruction that the person accused of crime is presumed to have intended the ordinary consequences of his or her voluntary acts. What has been the opinion of the Supreme Court of the United States concerning this type of instruction? (§6.12)

16. The presumption of law that a person is presumed to know the general public laws of his or her state of residence and of the United States has been stated by many courts as indicative of public policy. What is the effect of this presumption? (§6.13)

17. When should a judge offer a jury instruction covering a defendant's unexplained flight from a crime scene? Does proof of flight give rise to a presumption of consciousness of guilt? (§6.14)

18. Under what circumstances does it constitute an appropriate occasion for a judge to offer a jury instruction concerning the absence of a person from the usual environs as giving rise to a presumption or inference that the absent person is deceased? (§6.15)

19. Under what section of the United States Constitution is the presumption usually challenged? What is the opinion of the Supreme Court concerning statutory presumptions? (§6.17)

20. The parties involved in a criminal case may stipulate the existence or nonexistence of a fact. Does this exclude evidence regarding the truth or falsity of the matter stipulated? Give an example of a stipulation. (§6.18)

21. In *Kentucky v. Whorton*, the trial court, after a request by defense counsel, refused to instruct the jury on the presumption of innocence. What was the opinion of the Kentucky Supreme Court and later the United States Supreme Court regarding the trial court's failure to give a specific instruction on the presumption of innocence? (*Kentucky v. Whorton*) (§6.8)

22. In the case of *State v. Jackson*, the defendant was convicted of attempted burglary and appealed to the Supreme Court of Washington. One of the issues presented on appeal was whether, in an attempted burglary case, it is error to instruct the jury that it may infer that the defendant acted with intent to commit a crime within a building from the fact that the defendant may have attempted to enter the building. What was the decision of the court relating to this issue? What was the rationale of the court in regard to the constitutionality of criminal statutory presumptions? (*State v. Jackson*, Part II)

23. In *Illinois v. Purcell*, the defendant complained that the presumption of innocence was not being fully recognized since his pretrial bail. According to the state statute, bail may not be obtained where "the proof is evident or the presumption great" that the defendant committed a capital offense or an offense for which he may be sentenced to life imprisonment. May a state have a presumption of innocence for trial purposes and at the same time maintain that a defendant must prove innocence or at least prove that the evidence of his guilt was not strong in order to obtain pretrial release on bail? (*Illinois v. Purcell*, Part II)

Chapter 7
Relevancy and Materiality

Objectives

Because the primary objective and purpose in a criminal trial is to determine the truth regarding the issues presented, under the general rule all evidence is presumptively admissible. As the justice system developed in England and evolved in the United States, rudimentary rules admitting or excluding evidence experienced expanded development with a goal of allowing evidence for judge or jury consideration that assisted in the discovery of the truth. At the same time, some types of evidence became subject to rules of exclusion that had the effect of protecting various personal and societal interests that might have a higher value than merely illuminating the truth. At present, the rules of evidence have evolved into a complicated set of evidence rules governing the type of evidence that is presented to the trier of fact. To protect the accused, obstacles or requirements have been erected to filter out evidence that could improperly influence the jury. Two of these legal obstacles are: (1) the evidence must be relevant, and (2) the evidence must be material. A slightly different manner of phrasing these first two legal obstacles or requirements is to say that the evidence: (1) must be logically relevant and (2) that the evidence must also be legally relevant. A third obstacle, competency, is discussed in Chapter 8.

The general objective of this chapter is first to explain the procedure used in challenging the introduction of evidence; second, to define relevancy and materiality; and third, to give examples of situations in which the introduction of the evidence is challenged under the relevancy and materiality rules.

The objectives of this chapter are to:

1. Explain the procedure that is followed when an objection is made because the evidence is irrelevant, immaterial, or incompetent.

2. Define and distinguish the terms *relevancy* and *materiality.*

3. Explain the concepts of *logical relevancy* and *legal relevancy.*

4. Understand the role of the trial judge in entertaining objections to the admission of evidence; comprehend how the judge considers opposing legal rationales in making the decision, and appreciate the thought processes and legal rules followed by the judge in rendering a decision admitting or excluding evidence.

5. List five rationales for excluding relevant and material evidence and be able to give an example of each rationale.

6. Understand the five-factor test of *Neil v. Biggers*, designed to produce relevant personal identification evidence concerning suspects.

7. Address the relevancy rules relating to the identity of persons and the identity of physical objects at the trial.

8. Understand the relevancy of evidence that explains the conduct of a defendant prior to the commission of the crime that may assist in proving guilt by the prosecution or may be relevant to disprove guilt by the defendant.

9. Explain the relevancy rules applicable to the introduction of evidence of circumstances that occur subsequent to the crime.

10. Enable the student to understand that the requirement of relevancy applies to all evidence introduced by either party and applies to the admission of oral testimony and physical objects.

11. Evidence that purports to support theories of defense or innocence offered by a defendant must meet the tests of relevancy and materiality.

12. List and discuss the relevancy rules that are peculiar to the use of evidence concerning character, reputation, and evidence of other crimes committed by a witness or by the defendant.

13. Understand the requirements of relevancy and materiality with respect to the admissibility of the results of scientific tests, experiments, and demonstrations.

14. List the requirements for admissibility of scientific evidence under the *Daubert* standard as applied to trials in federal court.

Discussion Outline

§7.1   Introduction

§7.2   Relevancy and Materiality Defined
      A.   Relevant Evidence
      B.   Material Evidence
      C.   Materiality and Relevancy Distinguished

§7.3   Admissibility of Relevant Evidence
      A.   Federal Rule Concerning Admissibility
      B.   The General Relevancy Rule
      C.   The Trial Judge's Decision as to Relevancy

Review Questions

1. What procedure is followed in court in challenging evidence that is irrelevant, immaterial, or incompetent? (§7.1)

2. Distinguish between materiality and relevancy and give some examples of each. (§7.2)

3. Explain how the concepts of logical relevancy and legal relevancy relate to the traditional concepts of relevancy and materiality. (§7.2)

4. What is the general rule concerning the admissibility of relevant evidence? Who makes the decision as to relevancy? (§7.3)

5. While relevant evidence is presumptively admissible, many legal theories will result in the exclusion of relevant evidence for a variety of reasons, some logical and some based on public policy. What are some of the instances in which Federal Rule 403 may exclude relevant evidence from admission in court? (§7.4)

6. What is the general rule concerning the relevancy and materiality of evidence tending to establish the identity of persons involved in crimes? May "other crimes" evidence be used for identification purposes? (§7.6)

7. Under the *Neil v. Biggers* test for witness identification, what are the constitutional requirements that must be met in order to allow the admissibility of evidence of a victim's or witness's pretrial identification of the defendant from photographs or a lineup? (§7.6)

8. Will courts generally admit physical objects, forensic evidence, and other tangible evidence against a defendant? Is there a general rule concerning the admissibility of evidence of objects and scientific evidence connected to the crime? (§7.7)

9. Is evidence of conduct of the accused shortly *before* the offense, which is either consistent with innocence or consistent with a defendant's guilt considered relevant and admissible? If so, what are the limitations concerning the admissibility of such evidence? (§7.8)

10. Under what circumstances is evidence of conduct *following* the criminal act relevant? How relevant would the use of a false name, refusal to allow police to enter, or giving a false address be relevant in a criminal prosecution? (§7.9)

11. Why might evidence of fleeing the scene or flight after the crime be indicative of guilt? Why is flight following a crime not always relevant evidence of a consciousness of guilt? (§7.9)

12. Under what circumstances is evidence of insanity relevant and admissible? Voluntary intoxication? (§7.10)

13. Generally, evidence of a person's character or a trait of his character is not admissible for the purpose of proving that the defendant acted in the predicted manner on the occasion in question. Under Federal Rule 404(a), there are several exceptions mentioned. Define these exceptions to the general rule and explain the circumstances under which these exceptions apply. (§7.11)

14. Concerning the relevancy of allowing a prosecutor to introduce evidence of a defendant's prior criminal activities, The Court of Appeals for the Eleventh Circuit suggested following a two-step approach in determining the admissibility of evidence of other crimes. What is this two-step test? Enumerate at least four purposes for which evidence of other crimes is admissible. Discuss the rationale for admitting such evidence. (§7.12)

15. What factors did the *Daubert v. Merrell Dow* case suggest as appropriate for testing relevance in the admission of scientific evidence in federal court? Give an example of the use of experimental and scientific evidence as meeting the relevancy test. (§7.13)

16. The defendant in the case of *Massachusetts v. Prashaw* contended that the introduction of naked photographs of her in sexually provocative poses, during a case involving firearms violations, created unfair prejudice to her defense and that the photographs were not relevant in any sense to the theory of guilt proffered by the prosecution. Did the appellate court agree with the defendant or did it believe that the provocative photographs were relevant to the proof of the prosecution's case? Should the court have decided this case in the manner in which it did? Why or why not? (*Massachusetts v. Prashaw*, Part II)

17. In the case of *State v. Davis*, a jury found the defendant guilty of first degree murder. At the trial, evidence was introduced that, prior to the death of the victim, the defendant expressed a desire to kill three young women and have sexual relations with them while they were dying. On appeal, the defendant claimed that the introduction under Rule 404(b) of this evidence of conduct preceding the crimes should not have been admitted. What was the decision of the court concerning the admissibility of evidence of separate crimes? The admissibility of uncharged misconduct? Were the statements properly admitted? Why? Were the photographs of the autopsy of the victim properly admitted? Would the prejudicial value outweigh the probative effect? Why or why not? (*State v. Davis*, Part II)

18. The defendant in the case of *State v. Lancaster* claimed that he was entitled to a new trial because the state introduced inadmissible evidence of the commission of uncharged crimes. The state had offered the testimony of two other women who recounted numerous incidents of sexual abuse at the hands of the defendant. What was the decision of the court concerning the introduction of evidence of other similar crimes? The court noted five instances in which evidence of uncharged misconduct may be admitted as a general rule. What are they? (*State v. Lancaster*, Part II)

Chapter 8
Competency of Evidence and Witnesses

Objectives

Evidence that is competent, relevant, and material is admissible. Where evidence meets the relevancy and materiality tests, it must also be legally competent if it is to be considered by the jury or judge. Wrongfully obtained evidence, statutorily incompetent evidence, and evidence excluded due to court decision or established rules are all considered inadmissible under general concepts of incompetency. Even where the evidence is competent under the established rules, the witnesses who have been selected to present the evidence must also be considered competent or they will not be permitted to testify. The purpose of this chapter is twofold: (1) to analyze the rules relating to the competency of evidence, and (2) to consider the rules that bear on the competency of the prospective witnesses to testify. Included in the latter category are the competency of the judge and the competency of jurors as witnesses.

The objectives of this chapter are to:

1. Set the stage for an understanding of the rules relating to the competency of evidence and the competency of the witnesses.

2. Define *competency* and *incompetency*.

3. Give an example of incompetent evidence that has been wrongfully obtained.

4. Explain what is meant by the term *statutory incompetency* and be able to give an example.

5. Offer an example of when evidence is generally excluded on the basis of incompetency due to a rule of a court rule or a rule of evidence.

6. Examine the evidence rules that relate to various types of evidence such as documentary evidence and telephone conversations.

7. Understand how the federal test for competency of scientific tests and experiments changed following the case of *Daubert v. Merrell Dow Pharmaceuticals*.

8. Explain the necessity for laying a foundation for the use of canine evidence as a way of ensuring that the evidence will be deemed competent and admissible.

9. Detail the general requirements for assuring the competency of telephone conversations by establishing the reliability of the collection of the evidence and authentication of the identity of the speaker.

10. Discuss the rules relating to the use of negative evidence, i.e., evidence that a witness *did not* see or hear anything at the time of the incident.

11. Consider the principles that hold that evidence is competent for some purposes but not for others.

12. Distinguish between competency of evidence and competency of witnesses.

13. List the four elements of witness competency and explain the importance of each.

14. Understand that when determining a child's competency to testify, an oath to tell the truth will not be considered one of the elements of competency.

15. Trace the history and reasons for the common law rule that a husband and wife are incompetent as witnesses for or against each other and note that the modern rule has been altered in most jurisdictions.

16. Understand that a husband or a wife may be considered incompetent to testify concerning confidential matters communicated during the marriage and that the incompetency lasts beyond the duration of the marriage.

17. Understand that under modern law, a person who has been convicted of crime does not lose competency by virtue of the conviction, but that in the past, conviction of a crime could render the convicted person incompetent to testify in a court of law.

18. State the modern rule relating to the effect of a religious belief (or lack thereof) on the competency of a witness to testify.

19. Comprehend that under most modern evidence codes, including the Federal Rules of Evidence, judges and jurors are deemed incompetent to testify in the trial in which the judge is presiding or the juror is sitting.

Discussion Outline

§8.1   Introduction

§8.2   Definitions
    A. Competent Evidence
    B. Incompetent Evidence

Review Questions

1. Define *competent evidence* and *incompetent evidence* and give examples of each. (§8.2)

2. If evidence is found to be incompetent, it is usually because the courts have determined that it falls within one of three general categories. Name these three and give examples of evidence that would fall within each of the categories. (§8.3)

3. Why is illegally obtained evidence excluded from use at criminal trials under the concept of incompetency? (§8.3)

4. Is documentary evidence subject to the same competency rules as oral testimony? (§8.4)

5. What additional tests must documentary evidence pass in order to be considered competent? (§8.4)

6. In the federal courts, scientific tests, experiments, and demonstrations must meet the requirements set forth in *Daubert v. Merrell Dow Pharmaceuticals*. What are the standards that produce competent scientific evidence under the *Daubert* case? (§8.5)

7. To prove that the defendant committed an offense, evidence is often admitted concerning the events that led to his or her apprehension, such as the conduct of a dog trained to uncover illegal drugs. What foundation is necessary to prove that such evidence is competent? (§8.6)

8. How may a telephone conversation be authenticated in order to be considered competent evidence? (§8.7)

9. Explain the concept of negative evidence. A witness may testify generally as to what he or she saw or heard, but may the witness testify concerning what he or she did not hear or did not see? If so, under what conditions? (§8.8)

10. What are the four elements of competency for adults to qualify as witnesses? Explain. (§8.10)

11. Can illegally seized evidence be considered competent and admissible for some purposes and not for others? (§8.9)

12. Does the fact that a witness was formerly committed to a mental hospital necessarily render his or her testimony incompetent? Discuss. Who has the burden of proving mental incapacity? What is the test? (§8.11)

13. What are the elements of competency for a child to be considered available to testify? Is there a fixed age at which a child becomes a competent witness? Discuss. (§8.12)

14. What was the rationale for the common law rule that a wife was incompetent to testify as a witness for or against her husband? Under modern rules, can one spouse testify against the other? Do exceptions exist? (§8.13)

15. Does a criminal conviction have any effect on the competency of a witness to testify? Does it make any difference what type of crime the witness was convicted of? Explain. (§8.14)

16. Does the religious faith or absence of religious affinity have any effect on the competency of a witness? Does the opposing attorney have the right to challenge the testimony of a witness by bringing up the religious faith of the witness? Discuss. (§8.15)

17. Under Federal Rule of Evidence 605, may a judge who presides at a trial testify as a witness in that trial? Has this federal rule been adopted by the states? Discuss. (§8.16)

18. Should a juror be incompetent to testify in a case in which he or she is sitting as a juror? Would this create problems during deliberations? (§8.17)

19. In *Gillars v. United States*, the defendant was convicted of treason and appealed on the ground, among others, that a witness was incompetent because he stated that he did not believe in the God of the Bible. What was the decision of the court of appeals in regard to the competency of a witness who does not believe in God to testify? (*Gillars v. United States*, Part II)

20. In *Ohio v. Wells*, the trial court allowed a five year-old alleged victim to testify against a man accused of rape. The trial court conducted a hearing to determine the competency of the five-year-old and determined that she was competent as a witness to testify against defendant Wells. What did the appellate court determine concerning her competency to testify? What factors did the court consider in determining whether the child met the requirements of competency as a witness? (*Ohio v. Wells*, Part II)

21. The defendants in the case of *United States v. Phibbs* were convicted of drug distribution and conspiracy. On appeal, they claimed that two witnesses were incompetent to give testimony because of mental incapacity. What did the reviewing court decide concerning the exclusion of the testimony of a witness who has psychiatric problems? What is the test for determining mental qualification to testify? How does credibility of testimony fit into the picture? (*United States v. Phibbs*, Part II)

Chapter 9
Examination of Witnesses

Objectives

All evidence in criminal trials arrives through the testimony of witnesses who either directly testify to the historical facts or provide testimony that identifies or authenticates physical evidence, allowing it to be introduced to the trier of fact. Therefore, most of the evidence available in any case is the result of the oral testimony of witnesses. Before witnesses testify, however, they must be qualified in accordance with the evidentiary rules passed by the legislatures or promulgated by the courts. Even when witnesses have qualified to testify, the process of introducing this testimony is technical and often confusing because additional rules apply to regulate the content of what a witness says or is prohibited from mentioning.

The purpose of this chapter is to develop an understanding of the complicated rules relating to the qualities of the witness, the procedure followed in examining witnesses, and the methods of impeaching or discrediting witnesses.

The objectives of this chapter are to:

1. Learn the essential requirements for witness competency.

2. Clarify the oath or affirmation requirements.

3. Understand the general witness requirement of firsthand knowledge

4. Comprehend the discretion possessed by the judge in determining witness competency.

5. Examine the role of the judge in controlling the testimony of the witness.

6. Explain the reasons for excluding and separating witnesses during the trial and understand the exceptions to this principle.

7. Explain the purposes, goals, and procedure involved in direct examination of a witness.

8. Consider the rules relating to the use of leading questions on direct examination, and list the best-known exceptions to the rule that states that leading questions cannot be used on direct examination.

9. Understand why interrogation on direct examination may be directed toward hostile witnesses, adverse parties, or a witnesses whose interests are allied with an adverse party.

10. Explain the difference between *present memory revived* and *past recollection recorded* and understand why the latter is considered a hearsay exception.

11. Define the scope of cross-examination and understand that different jurisdictions have different limitations concerning the scope.

12. List the three reasons for authorizing leading questions when examining an opposing party's witness.

13. Learn the purposes and scope of redirect examination and recross-examination.

14. Define "impeachment" and explain the impeachment process.

15. Understand the traditional rule that prohibits the impeachment of one's own witness and the modern rule permitting the impeachment of any witness by any party.

16. Name and explain the primary means of impeaching witnesses, including bias or prejudice, interest, character, conviction of a crime, confession, prior inconsistent statements, and defects of recollection and perception.

17. Using case situations, examine the law relating to the use of the confession in the impeachment of witnesses.

18. Discuss how a witness, once impeached, can be rehabilitated through redirect examination.

Discussion Outline

§9.1   Introduction

§9.2   Essential Qualities of a Witness
      A.   Personal Connection with the Relevant Occurrence
      B.   Mental and Physical Faculties Sufficient to Observe the Events
      C.   Ability to Recollect and Relate Events to the Jury
      D.   Ability to Communicate

§9.3   Oath or Affirmation Requirement
      A.   Rule 603, Federal Rules of Evidence
      B.   Expression of a Religious Belief not Required
      C.   Oath Not Required of Children

§9.14   —Bias or Prejudice
         A.   Great Latitude in Pursuing
         B.   Includes Adverse Interests, Affiliation, Motive to Fabricate

§9.15   —Character and Conduct
         A.   Federal Rule 608
         B.   Requirements

§9.16   —Conviction of Crime
         A.   General Rule Concerning Introduction of Evidence of Other Crimes for
              Impeachment
         B.   When Other Crimes or Misconduct May Be Used for Impeachment

§9.17   —Prior Inconsistent Statements
         A.   General Rule
         B.   Interpretation of Rule 613, Federal Rules of Evidence

§9.18   —Defects of Recollection or Perception
         A.   Sight, Hearing, or Smell
         B.   Not in a Position to Have Firsthand Perception

§9.19   —Use of Confession for Impeachment Purposes
         A.   Must Have Been Voluntary and Freely Given
         B.   Need Not Meet *Miranda* Requirements.

§9.20   Rehabilitation of Witness

§9.21   Summary

Review Questions

1. What are the essential qualities of a competent witness? (§9.2)

2. Rule 603 of the Federal Rules of Evidence requires that, before testifying, a witness shall be required to declare that he or she will testify truthfully by oath or affirmation. Does this mean that the witness must declare a belief in God? What is the purpose of the oath or affirmation? (§9.3)

3. What part does the judge play in guiding the testimony of a witness? Is the judge's authority unlimited? Explain. (§9.4)

4. What is meant by "separation of witnesses?" What is the rationale for separating witnesses? (§9.5)

5. Why are some potential witnesses excluded from the order sequestering witnesses during the testimony of other witnesses? (§9.5)

6. Are police officers who have investigated a case always excluded from the courtroom as other witnesses are? Why or why not? (§9.5)

7. What is meant by the term *direct examination of witnesses*? Which party conducts the direct examination? (§9.6)

8. Define the term *leading question*. What are the rules for using leading questions on direct examination? What factors are considered in determining whether a witness is hostile? (§9.7)

9. There are at least four exceptions to the rule prohibiting leading questions on direct examination. Name these exceptions and give the rationale for each. (§9.7)

10. Distinguish between the concepts of *present memory revived* and *past recollection recorded*. Why is past recollection recorded considered a hearsay exception? When is a witness authorized to use a writing to refresh memory? (§§9.8, 9.9)

11. What is meant by "hypnotically refreshed testimony?" Does this technique qualify as present memory refreshed? May such testimony be admitted in a criminal case? If so, what are the requirements? (§9.8)

12. Name three reasons for authorizing leading questions when examining the opposing party's witness. (§9.10)

13. What are the general goals or purposes of conducting cross-examination of the adverse party's witnesses? (§9.10)

14. Why are leading questions allowed on cross-examination but only rarely permitted on direct examination? (§9.10)

15. After a witness has been cross-examined by opposing counsel, the party calling the witness may ask additional questions. What is this called? What is the scope of such an examination? (§9.11)

16. What is the general purpose of impeaching an adverse party's witness? (§9.12)

17. What is the general rule concerning the impeachment of a witness? Give three approved methods of impeaching a witness. (§9.12)

18. In what way does every witness place his or her credibility at issue by becoming a trial witness? (§9.12)

19. Under what conditions may a party impeach its own witness? May the government impeach its own witness? (§9.13)

20. List five ways of discrediting or impeaching a witness and explain the conditions under which they may be used. (§9.14-9.18)

21. May the credibility of a witness be attacked or supported by opinion or reputation evidence? If so, what are the limitations? (§9.15)

22. May the credibility of a witness be attacked by introducing evidence that that witness has committed a crime? If so, what types of crimes may be referred to and for what purpose? Does it make any difference if the witness was pardoned? (§9.16)

23. May the testimony of a witness be impeached by showing that the witness gave inconsistent declarations, statements, or testimony? If such testimony is allowed, what rights are afforded the opposing party? (§9.17)

24. In order to be used for impeachment purposes, must a confession have been offered freely and voluntarily by the witness in order to be admitted against him or her? (§9.19)

25. Confessions may sometimes be used for impeachment purposes even though they may not be used for the prosecutor's evidence in chief. What is the reason for allowing the use of a confession for impeachment even though the *Miranda* warnings were not given? (§9.19)

26. May the prosecution introduce evidence at the trial that indicates that the defendant failed to give the police exculpatory statements after being arrested? Explain. (§9.19)

27. What is meant by *rehabilitation of a witness*? (§9.20)

28. In *United States v. Drummond*, the trial court refused to require the government's case agent to testify first so that he would not have the benefit of hearing all the other government witnesses give their testimony before the case agent gave his evidence. Because witnesses can be excluded from the courtroom prior to giving testimony, could the trial judge have ordered the case agent for the prosecution to leave the courtroom? Why or why not? Why not require the case agent to testify first so that he could not tailor his testimony? Would such an order have been fair to both parties? (*United States v. Drummond*, Part II)

29. In *Isler v. United States*, in which the defendant had been accused of murder, the trial court allowed the reading of a witness's grand jury statement to the jury. There had been a prior trial at which time the witnesses, who now are without any memory of the homicide, testified. The witnesses were not subject to cross-examination at the grand jury proceeding, but were cross-examined at the first trial. Did the present trial court correctly rule that past recollection recorded could be used at a subsequent trial over the defendant's objection that he was prevented from cross-examining the witnesses? How did the appellate court rule? Would you have decided the case any differently? Why? (*Isler v. United States*, Part II)

30. In *United States v. Spivey*, the trial court refused to allow the defendant's counsel to conduct an unlimited Sixth Amendment cross-examination of prosecution witnesses, and one witness in particular. The defense counsel attempted to bring every possible impeachment-oriented factor of one of the government's witnesses out on cross-examination and was moving methodically and slowly. Finally, the trial judge would not permit any more cross-examination. Under the circumstances, did the defendant suffer from a failure of the judge to allow additional cross-examination? What were the judge's reasons for concluding cross-examination? Do the rules of evidence regulate cross-examination? Was Spivey's conviction reversed? (*United States v. Spivey*, Part II)

31. In *Griffin v. Georgia*, the trial court allowed the defendant's girlfriend to testify that the defendant had not beaten her, but that she had fallen in a drunken stupor and hit her head on a concrete barrier outside the apartment that she shared with the defendant. The court permitted evidence of her 911 call, in which she stated that the defendant had attacked her, and police officers were permitted to testify that she had told them that the defendant had beaten her. The defendant, Griffin, objected to the admission of the prior inconsistent statements as both impeachment devices and as substantive evidence. Should the trial court have admitted her prior inconsistent statements on the 911 tape to impeach her because she was a prosecution witness? Should her prior statements to the police who responded to the 911 call be admitted as prior inconsistent statements? What did the appellate court decide concerning the admissibility of the prior inconsistent statement evidence? (*Griffin v. Georgia*, Part II)

Chapter 10
Privileges

Objectives

In a criminal case, the courts seek the truth, but rules of evidence have always been concerned not only with the truth, but also with the manner of ascertaining the truth. Nevertheless, any limitations on the admissibility of evidence that tend to stifle the truth must be limited and carefully defined.

In this chapter, certain privileged communications, such as attorney-client, physician-patient, and husband-wife, are discussed, and the complex rules surrounding these privileges are explained. The objective is to make certain that the reader understands the reasons for these privileged communications and, more importantly, the exceptions to the privilege rules.

The objectives of this chapter are to:

1. Explain the two general privilege rules and trace the development of the rules.

2. Weigh the desire to protect personal relationships against the need to ascertain the truth in a criminal case.

3. State the rule that protects some communications between husband and wife and delineate the exceptions to the general rule.

4. Define the attorney-client privilege, the scope of the privilege and the specific exceptions.

5. Trace the development of the rule that protects communications between physician and patient and expound on the scope of the rule, the exceptions, and how the privilege is claimed and waived.

6. State the statutory rule relating to communications to clergy, and discuss the scope of the privilege where there is a statute, the admissibility of information confided where there is no statute, and the waiver provisions.

7. Clarify the confusion that exists about the confidential informant privilege.

8. Explain the principle that protects state secrets and other official information, and consider the effect of the principle in criminal cases.

9. Examine statutes and court decisions relating to the news media-informant privilege.

Discussion Outline

§10.1   Introduction

§10.2   Reasons for Privileged Communications

§10.3   Communications between Husband and Wife
    A.   Statement of the Rules
    B.   Scope of the Privilege
    C.   Exceptions
    D.   Duration of the Privilege

§10.4   Communications between Attorney and Client
    A.   Statement of the Rule
    B.   Scope of the Privilege
    C.   Exceptions
    D.   Assertion and Waiver

§10.5   Communications between Physician and Patient
    A.   Statement of the Rule
    B.   Scope of the Privilege
    C.   Exceptions
    D.   Assertion and Waiver

§10.6   Communications to Clergy
    A.   Statement of the Rule
    B.   Scope of the Privilege
    C.   Exceptions
    D.   Assertion and Waiver

§10.7   Confidential Informant Privilege

§10.8   State Secrets and Other Official Information

§10.9   News Media-Informant Privilege

§10.10   Summary

Review Questions

1. When considering privileged communications, there are two rules. What are they? What is the rationale for the courts' reluctance to expand the privilege?

2. What is the rationale for the testimonial privilege that declares some evidence, although relevant, to be inadmissible in criminal cases?

3. Is the husband-wife privilege the same now as it was 50 years ago? If not, discuss its development. What four tests are applied in claiming the privilege? Does the privilege extend to homosexuals in "spousal relationships?"

4. State and give examples of three exceptions to the husband-wife privilege.

5. Does the husband-wife privilege extend to statements made during marriage if the trial takes place after a divorce? Explain. Does the same rule apply if the parties are separated but not divorced?

6. Briefly state the attorney-client privilege and give the rationale for the privilege.

7. Name the exceptions to the attorney-client privilege and give the reasons for each exception. What is meant by the *crime-fraud* exception? Discuss the two-point test that governs this exception. Does the privilege survive the death of the client?

8. Who has the legal power to assert the attorney-client privilege? Are there any exceptions? Explain.

9. What is the physician-patient privilege? What is its primary purpose? What are the exceptions? Does the privilege apply to communications with a psychologist? Other relationships? Explain.

10. Is the rule that a person has a privilege to refuse to disclose confidential communications made to a clergy member a common law rule or a statutory rule? How does this affect the practical application of the rule?

11. Does the clergy member or the penitent have the right to claim or waive the privilege relating to communications to clergy? Explain.

12. Under what conditions does the state have the right to withhold from disclosure the identity of persons who furnish information to the police concerning the commission of a crime? Give some examples.

13. What is the policy basis of the rule that certain state secrets are privileged?

14. What is the present status of the law relating to the news media-informant privilege?

15. What is meant by the term *shield law*, as used in considering the news media-informant privilege? What is the intent behind shield laws? Under what conditions must the privilege give way to countervailing interests?

16. In *Trammel v. United States*, the defendant was convicted of importing heroin and conspiring to import heroin. He appealed on the ground that the trial court committed reversible error by allowing his wife to testify against him. What was the decision of the reviewing court in regard to the wife being permitted to testify adversely in a criminal case?

17. The defendant broke into her ex-husband's house and shot her ex-husband and his girlfriend. The girlfriend was killed and the ex-husband was injured. The defendant was charged with first-degree murder and attempted murder (*State v. Hardin*). The defendant was convicted of first degree murder and willful injury and appealed. The reviewing court considered and discussed the physician-patient privilege. What did the decision disclose concerning: (1) whether the privilege is a common law privilege or a statutory privilege; (2) the exceptions to the physician-patient privilege; and (3) the right of a defendant to have counsel present at a psychiatric evaluation?

18. In the case of *State v. Demarco,* the issue was whether the state may compel discovery of reports prepared by the defendant's expert witness for other clients in unrelated cases. In the discussion, the court considered the application of the attorney-client privilege to materials prepared by agents of the attorney retained to aid in the preparation of the case. What is the *work product* doctrine? Does the attorney-client privilege apply when the attorney for the defendant retains a scientific expert to aid in the preparation of the defense? Does the Sixth Amendment right to assistance of counsel have any relationship to the attorney-client and work product privileges?

Chapter 11
Opinions and Expert Testimony

Objectives

Trial witnesses traditionally are limited to giving answers that contain only facts and are not theoretically supposed to render opinions because the function of the jury is to evaluate the evidence and develop opinions and conclusions regarding the factual matters at issue. Practical necessity has dictated that exceptions to this rule must be recognized. As a logical proposition, many items of evidence that seem to contain facts actually contain opinions to a greater or lesser degree. The statement of a witness describing a color or explaining height may be an opinion rather than a clear statement of objective fact. The purpose of this chapter is to state, define, and give reasons for the rule, and to enumerate the many exceptions to the rule, excluding opinions and the requirements of the exceptions. The law of evidence treats expert witnesses differently from lay witnesses because expert witnesses are expected to offer opinions covering their respective areas of expertise. Because the requirements are different for experts and nonexperts, the materials in this chapter must, by necessity, distinguish between opinions given by experts and opinions offered by nonexperts. The chapter materials will discuss in detail the specific rules relating to the admission of opinion evidence and testimony.

The objectives of the chapter are to:

1. Introduce the student to the opinion testimony concept and explain the reason for the opinion rule.

2. Define terms used in connection with expert testimony such as *opinion evidence, expert witness,* and *nonexpert witness.*

3. Understand the limitations placed on the opinions of both lay and expert witnesses.

4. State the three requirements of Rule 701 that must be met before nonexperts may give opinions.

5. Enumerate some of the most common exceptions in which nonexpert opinions are admissible and explain the conditions that must be met before these opinions are admitted.

6. Understand the requirements that an expert witness must meet in order to offer expert opinion evidence.

7. Comprehend the areas of overlap concerning lay and expert opinions.

8. List the requirements for the use of expert testimony.

9. Define the procedure that is followed in qualifying a witness as an expert.

10. Describe the procedure that is followed in selecting an expert witness.

11. Develop an understanding that some facts, conclusions, and opinions can only be introduced through the use of a qualified expert witness.

12. Present the two avenues by which expert evidence may be presented to the jury or other fact finder.

13. Detail the procedure that is followed in cross-examining expert witnesses.

14. Enumerate some common examples of subjects of expert testimony along with the requirements for admission.

15. Explain the role of experts from crime laboratories.

16. Present cases to more thoroughly explain the application of the opinion evidence rule and to give examples of situations in which nonexpert and expert testimony are admissible in spite of the general opinion evidence rule.

Discussion Outline

§11.1   Introduction
    A. General Rule Relating to the Admissibility of Opinion Testimony
    B. Exceptions

§11.2   Definitions and Distinctions
    A. Opinion Evidence
    B. Expert Witness
    C. Nonexpert Witness

§11.3   Admissibility of Nonexpert Opinions
    A. General Rule Regarding Nonexpert Testimony
    B. Qualifications of Lay Witness in Presenting Opinion Testimony

§11.4   Subjects of Nonexpert Opinions
    A. Age
    B. Appearance
    C. Conduct
    D. Distance and Space

Review Questions

1. What is the general evidence rule relating to the admissibility of opinions of witnesses in a criminal case? Explain the rationale for this rule. (§§ 11.1, 11.3)

2. Explain the reasons for the exceptions to the opinion rule. (§11.1)

3. Define *opinion evidence, expert witness,* and *nonexpert witness.* (§11.2)

4. A nonexpert, or lay witness, may state a relevant opinion if three requirements are met. What are the three requirements? What is the effect of Federal Rule 701? May a witness give an explanation regarding the defendant's guilt? (§11.3)

5. Explain how a lay witness may offer opinions on the same subject as an expert witness. (§11.2)

6. A nonexpert witness is asked, "What was the appearance of the man at the time, with reference to his being rational or irrational?" Will an answer be allowed over the objection of the other party? Explain. (§11.4)

7. May a layperson give an opinion in identifying another's handwriting? If so, what are the requirements? (§11.4(I))

8. What kind of foundation would have to be developed for a lay witness to offer an opinion that a person was intoxicated? (§11.4)

9. A police officer testified, "In my opinion, the defendant was drunk." Under what conditions is this nonexpert opinion testimony admissible? Do the same rules apply in drug cases? (§11.4(F)) May a nonexpert give an opinion regarding mental condition? What are the requirements? (§11.4(G))

10. Rule 702 of the Federal Rules of Evidence defines the conditions under which expert testimony is admissible. What is the general rule relating to the use of expert testimony? (§11.5)

11. How does one qualify as an expert witness? (§11.6)

12. Can a witness qualify as an expert when he or she does not have a degree or license? May the special knowledge necessary to qualify as an expert be derived from experience? May the fact that the expert does not have a degree or license be brought out at the trial? (§11.6)

13. How does the defense attorney or prosecutor go about selecting an expert witness and having him or her qualified by the court? (§11.7)

14. There are two avenues through which expert evidence may be presented to a jury. Briefly state these and explain the differences between them. (§11.8)

15. When an expert witness takes the stand, may his or her opinions be challenged in the cross-examination process? What is the process for challenging these opinions? (§11.9)

16. Common subjects of expert testimony are the physical and mental condition of a person. Is it necessary that the expert in such situations be a person licensed to practice medicine? If not, what are the qualifications? (§11.10(C))

17. When an expert gives an opinion regarding handwriting, must he or she state that he or she is positive that the samples are identical? Does requiring a suspect to give a handwriting specimen violate the Fifth Amendment? (§11.10(E))

18. Why do most courts exclude expert testimony explaining the results of polygraph examinations? Can polygraph examiners be qualified as expert witnesses? When can polygraph examination results be admitted into evidence through the use of expert testimony? (§11.10(G))

19. How does a witness qualify as an expert in a drug case? May a police officer testify as an expert witness when the case involves drug violations? (§11.10(K))

20. Under what conditions may those who conduct a test in a crime laboratory testify concerning the significance of the test? (§11.11)

21. A defendant was charged with driving under the influence and resisting arrest. At the trial, over the objection of the defendant, a lay witness was allowed to testify that, based on what he observed, "the defendant was intoxicated." One of the issues on appeal was "did the district court err in admitting lay witness opinion testimony?" What was the provision of Rule 701 of the Montana rules of evidence? Did the rule preclude a lay witness from testifying about a person's state of intoxication? What was the conclusion of the Supreme Court of Montana concerning the admission of the lay witness testimony in this case? (*State v. Carter*, Part II)

22. The state of Texas charged a defendant with possession of a recreational amount of marijuana and he was convicted. A police officer had noticed marijuana during a routine traffic stop and arrested Osbourn. To use an expert at trial, notice was required under the Texas law in force at the time of the trial. The trial court permitted the police officer to identify the leafy substance as marijuana after she noted that she had received drug training at the police academy. Should the police officer have been allowed to identify marijuana as a lay witness? Does it take an expert witness to be used to identify marijuana? Is this the type of evidence on which both lay and expert witness might be able to offer opinions? Explain. (*Osbourn v. Texas*, Part II)

23. In the case of *United States v. de Soto,* the defendants were charged with possession of cocaine with intent to distribute and with conspiring to distribute cocaine. At the trial, one of the police officers involved in the investigation was allowed to testify as an expert regarding: (1) his opinion on the manner in which drug deal-

ers operate; (2) his opinion on the true nature of certain activities that he observed; and (3) his interpretation of certain seized documents. After the defendants were convicted, they appealed, arguing that the court erred in allowing the officer to testify as an expert. What was the determination of the court concerning the:

(1) average person's knowledge of the clandestine manner in which drugs are bought and sold?

(2) authority of law enforcement officers to testify as experts in drug cases?

(3) practice concerning the reversal of lower court decisions in expert testimony situations?

(4) legality of authorizing a witness to testify both as an eyewitness to the events and an expert? (*United States v. de Soto*, Part II)

Chapter 12
Hearsay Rule and Exceptions

Objectives

Almost everyone has heard the term *hearsay*, but the precise legal definition often seems to be misunderstood. Hearsay evidence consists of an out-of-court statement that is offered in court to prove the truth of what it asserts. Where the out-of-court statement has not been offered in court for the truth of its contents, the statement is not considered hearsay. The failure of criminal justice personnel to understand the rule, and especially the exceptions to the rule can lead to poorly prepared criminal cases.

The objectives for this chapter include defining and explaining the hearsay rule, as well as tracing some of the history of the rule and its exceptions. This chapter emphasizes the practical application of the hearsay rule in developing and presenting testimony in criminal trials.

The objectives of this chapter are to:

1. Understand that, unless an exception to the hearsay rule applied, hearsay evidence is not admissible in court.

2. State and explain the four reasons for the hearsay rule.

3. Define the terms *statement, declarant, hearsay,* and other terms used in the Federal Rules of Evidence. Emphasize what statements are *not* hearsay.

4. Trace the history and development of the hearsay rule in England and the United States.

5. Give the general rationale for exceptions to the hearsay rule.

6. Understand why hearsay exceptions exist as well as the rationale for admitting hearsay evidence under exceptions to the rule.

7. Delineate the four conditions that must be met before the "spontaneous and excited utterances" exception applies.

8. Understand that under the "excited utterances" exception, the declarant's statement may be made some time after the startling event and that court determinations are not always in conformity.

9. Consider the purpose of the exception that authorizes the use of business and public records and explain the Uniform Business Records Act.

10. Understand that the term "business record" encompasses virtually any record compiled by a regularly conducted activity, and may include schools and drug trafficking organizations.

11. Examine the exception to the hearsay rule that permits the introduction of evidence of pedigree, genealogy, and family history.

12. Develop an understanding of "former testimony" as an exception to the general hearsay rule and define "unavailability" as used in Federal Rule 804.

13. Understand the theoretical basis for believing the truth of a dying declaration made by a dying declarant.

14. Discuss the requirements that must be met before a dying declaration is admitted.

15. Explain the essential difference between a declaration against interest and an admission or a confession.

16. Clarify the reason for the *declaration against interest* exception and give examples of the application of this exception; list factors to be considered in making the determination.

17. Discuss the rule authorizing the use of confessions and admissions although these are technically hearsay.

18. Delineate the three conditions stated in Rule 804 of the Federal Rules of Evidence that justify the use of hearsay evidence even though not specifically listed in the rules. State and explain the conditions that must exist when applying the "residual" exception provisions of Federal Rules 803 and 804.

19. Explain why nontestimonial utterances do not come within the scope of the hearsay rule. Give examples.

20. Using case situations, examine the rationale for the hearsay rule and its exceptions.

Discussion Outline

§12.11   —Other Exceptions
    A.   General Conditions for Miscellaneous Exceptions
    B.   Conditions for Application

§12.12   Nontestimonial Utterances
    A.   Definition
    B.   Examples

§12.13   Summary

Review Questions

1. Explain the rationale for excluding evidence under the hearsay rule. What is the hearsay rule? Define the following terms as they are used in relation to the admission of hearsay evidence: *statement, declarant, hearsay, statements that are not hearsay.* Give some examples of statements that are *not* hearsay. (§§12.1, 12.2)

2. What is the relationship between the history of the hearsay rule and the history of the trial by jury? (§12.3)

3. What four reasons are advanced as to why hearsay evidence should not be admitted? What is the rationale for allowing some hearsay evidence to be admitted? (§§12.1, 12.4)

4. Explain how the "spontaneous or excited utterance" operates. Why should a spontaneous utterance be believed as truthful? (§12.5)

5. State the four requirements that must be met if a spontaneous utterance is to be admitted as an exception to the rule. Give some examples. What part does time play in determining whether a statement is spontaneous? Does this apply if statements are made to police officers? (§12.5)

6. Why are business and public records usually admitted even though the person who originally made the records is not present? Give some examples of reports that are admissible under the exception. (§12.6)

7. What is the basis for the family history (pedigree) exception to the rule? Give some examples. (§12.7)

8. What is the rationale for admitting "former testimony" as an exception to the hearsay rule? Is it really hearsay by the definition? (§12.8)

9. Under what conditions may evidence relating to testimony given at a former trial be admitted into court? Who has the burden of proof to show that a witness is unavailable? What is the "unavailability" test? (§12.8)

10. What is a dying declaration? Must a declarant state that he or she is aware of imminent death before the statement is admissible? In what type of case is a dying declaration admissible? Are such statements admitted if elicited by questions? (§12.9)

11. Why are declarations against the interests of the declarant admissible as exceptions to the hearsay rule? Give some examples. (§12.10)

12. What is the rationale for allowing some confessions into evidence even though the confessions are hearsay? Are confessions reliable as hearsay exceptions? Does the defendant have a real complaint when the defendant made the confession? (§12.10)

13. What are "residual" exceptions to the hearsay rule? What inquiries are made to determine their admissibility? Explain their application. (§12.11)

14. When the physical or mental state of a person is to be proved, declarations of another that are indicative of the declarant's physical or mental state are admitted. Are such statements hearsay? For what purpose are such statements admitted? Discuss. Distinguish between out-of-court statements offered to prove the matter asserted and statements that are not hearsay. (§12.12)

15. In *Bell v. Florida*, the victim of an attempted kidnapping at gunpoint stated that she was walking along the street during the daytime when the defendant twice drove up to her in his van and offered to give her a ride to her destination. The defendant changed his location and accosted her by grabbing her around the neck, holding a gun to her head, and attempted to force her into his vehicle. When she broke free and ran into traffic, she pounded on cars and asked for help in getting away. The defendant, while standing nearby, pointed his gun in her direction and threatened to shoot her. When she managed to call police and talk to them at her residence, she was barely able to speak coherently. When she told her story to police, they remembered it sufficiently to testify about it at his trial. The defendant argued that the victim's statements failed to meet the excited utterance test because there was a time delay of approximately 50 minutes between the time of the incident and the time the victim became calm enough to speak. According to the defendant, this was sufficient time for the victim to contrive or misrepresent. What are the general requirements for the application of the excited utterance exception? Would the victim have had time for reason to return if it took 50 minutes for her to become coherent? Did the court approve of the admission of an excited utterance exception in this case? Do you agree with the court's decision? Why or why not? (*Bell v. Florida*, Part II)

16. Federal Rule of Evidence 801(d)(1)(B) provides that a witness's prior statements are not hearsay if they are consistent with the witness's testimony and offered to rebut a charge against the witness of "recent fabrication or improper influence or motive." In *Tome v. United States,* the defendant was convicted of sexual abuse of his daughter. The government claimed that the assault was committed while the defendant had custody of the child. The defendant countered that the allegations were concocted so the child would not be returned to him. The government pre-

sented six witnesses who recounted out-of-court statements made by the child after the charged fabrication. Does the rule permit introduction of a declarant's consistent out-of-court statements to rebut a charge of recent fabrication if the statements were made *after* the charged fabrication? Does the federal rule, as interpreted, differ from the common law rule? What was the decision of the court in this case? (*Tome v. United States*, Part II)

17. Upon responding to a domestic dispute radio call in *Cox v. Indiana*, officers observed defendant Cox standing in front of an apartment building talking to another police officer. One deputy found Cox's girlfriend inside an apartment building. He noticed that she was crying and shaking and appeared to be very upset. The officer also noticed that she was talking very quickly and showed signs of a fresh injury, including a cut above her eye that was bleeding; her left eye was swollen; and she was holding an ice pack to her eye. Additionally, she had marks on her neck that appeared to have been caused by someone grabbing her on the neck. Cox contended on appeal that the hearsay testimony of the deputy who told the court some of what the girlfriend told him while she was upset should have been ruled as inadmissible because it failed to fit into any hearsay exception and because his girlfriend did not appear as a witness at the trial. Cox also contended that, if the testimony fell under the excited utterance exception, the prosecution failed to lay a proper foundation for the evidence. Should the appellate court reverse the case because the excited utterance exception did not apply in this context? Why or why not? Did it seem that there was there a sufficiently startling event? How long would it take for a person who has just been beaten by her boyfriend to calm down? Did the evidence in the case indicate that she had returned to rational thought and contemplation? What kind of foundation for a spontaneous utterance could be made in this case? (*Cox v. Indiana*, Part II)

18. In the case of *Morgan v. Georgia*, the defendant, Morgan, and the deceased were visiting Morgan's girlfriend at her home. When Morgan and the soon-to-be-deceased began to argue over Morgan's rough treatment of his girlfriend, Morgan shot the other man. At the hospital, the victim told police that Morgan shot him and detailed the circumstances under which he had received the gunshot wounds. At the hospital, the victim told a police officer that Morgan "just shot me" and "we weren't fighting." The officer who took the statement testified that the victim exhibited great pain and asked the officer "if he was going to die." The officer told him that he was not going to die and that the doctor was working on him. Morgan contended that this testimony shows that the victim was not conscious of imminent death, and for that reason, the trial court erroneously admitted the victim's statement to police as a dying declaration. Was the victim conscious of his impending death? Was the victim unavailable to testify at trial? Does it make any difference that the deceased may not have stated clearly that he knew he was going to die? Did the victim have any motivation for lying to the police at the hospital? Is this a close case for the court to determine? Would you have ruled the same way as the appellate court? Why? (*Morgan v. Georgia*, Part II).

19. In the case of *Michigan v. Washington,* the defendant and an accomplice were convicted of armed robbery and assault with intent to do great bodily harm. Police stopped the two men for routine questioning. Later, they heard a radio report of a robbery and shooting. One of the men they stopped blurted out that he was the shooter. He was later identified as the shooter. Because the confessing partner was tried separately, the judge allowed his statement to be admitted in evidence against his partner, Washington, as a declaration against interest. Washington appealed his conviction, contending that the admission of his accomplice's declaration against interest should not have been used against him. How did the appellate court rule? What rationale did it use in making its decision? Were there sufficient guarantees of trustworthiness to allow the evidence to be admitted as an exception to the hearsay rule? Would you have ruled the same way as the appellate court? Why? (*Michigan v. Washington,* Part II).

Chapter 13
Documentary Evidence

Objectives

An important portion of evidence considered by triers of fact are written documents and other related items of evidence that are called writings even though they may not be documents in the usual sense. Documentary evidence considered by the court and jury in reaching a decision may include a traditional writing, a videotape, or an audiotape. The general requirements of relevance, materiality, and competency discussed in previous chapters relating to opinion testimony and the hearsay rule apply to documentary evidence as well as to oral testimony. However, there are some tests that are peculiar to documentary evidence, and the purpose of this chapter is to examine them, especially those relating to authentication and the best evidence rule.

The objectives of this chapter are to:

1. Define documentary evidence and compare documentary evidence with other categories.

2. Enumerate the requirements for authentication of documentary evidence.

3. Explain what is meant by *self-authentication* and give examples of documents that are usually considered self-authenticating. State and explain Federal Rules 901 and 902.

4. State and explain four methods of authenticating documents.

5. Designate specific types of documentary evidence and explain the limitations on the use of each type.

6. Describe the rule of evidence that states that the best evidence that is attainable in the circumstances of the case must be used to prove a disputed fact, and study decisions that give examples of the exceptions to the best evidence rule.

7. Indicate the circumstances in which secondary evidence is allowable if the original writing is not available and give examples of federal cases that interpret Federal Rule 1003.

8. By the use of case material, give examples of the rules relating to the use of summaries of voluminous documents.

9. Develop the principles relating to the admissibility and weight to be given to statements, books, and learned treatises.

10. Referring to specific cases, explore the process used by the courts in interpreting the best evidence rule as codified in the Federal Rules of Evidence and in state statutes.

Discussion Outline

§13.1   Introduction
         A.   Three Categories of Evidence
         B.   Definition of Documentary Evidence
         C.   Applicability of the General Rules of Evidence to Documentary Evidence

§13.2   Authentication
         A.   The Authentication Rule
         B.   Interpretation of Rule 901 of the Federal Rules of Evidence
         C.   Methods of Authentication
         D.   Authentication of Computer Printouts

§13.3   Self-Authentication
         A.   What Is Meant by Self-Authentication?
         B.   Ten Types of Writings That Are Considered Self-Authenticating Under the Federal Rules of Evidence
         C.   Cases Interpreting Rule 902

§13.4   Methods of Authentication
         A.   Laying the Foundation for Admissibility
         B.   Four Methods of Proof

§13.5   Specific Examples of Documentary Evidence
         A.   Public Records and Documents
         B.   Private Writings

§13.6   Best Evidence Rule
         A.   Statement of the Rule
         B.   Purposes and Reasons for the Rule
         C.   Interpretation of Federal Rule 1002

§13.7   Secondary Evidence
         A.   Definition of Secondary Evidence and Duplicates
         B.   Conditions Precedent to the Use of Secondary Evidence
         C.   Admissibility Under Federal Rule 1003
         D.   Use of Carbon Copies of Documents
         E.   Application of the Rule to Recordings and Photographs

§13.8   Summaries
    A. Definition of Summaries
    B. Conditions Precedent to the Use of Summaries
    C. Examples

§13.9   Learned Treatises

§13.10 Summary

Review Questions

1. Distinguish documentary evidence, oral testimony, and real evidence. (§13.1)

2. Do rules of evidence, with respect to relevancy, competency, and materiality, apply to documentary evidence as they apply in the case of oral testimony? What other tests are peculiar to the use of documentary evidence? (§13.1)

3. What is meant by the statement that documentary evidence is not admissible until it has been authenticated? Must evidence that is introduced to authenticate a document be direct evidence? Explain. (§13.2)

4. What is meant by self-authentication? Explain Federal Rule 902 and give examples of evidence conforming with this rule. List five types of writings that are considered self-authenticating under Rule 902 of the Federal Rules of Evidence. (§13.3)

5. Unless documents are self-authenticating, a foundation must be established for admissibility. There are four methods of proof. Name three of them. How is the foundation established? (§13.4)

6. What is the rationale for admitting evidence from official records and public documents even though the person who made the documents is not testifying? (§13.5)

7. Death certificates and certified autopsy reports are generally received in evidence. What parts of such reports may be challenged? (§13.5)

8. What is the best evidence rule? Why have the courts adopted it? What are the provisions of Federal Rule 1002? (§13.6)

9. What proof must be offered in court as a condition of the admissibility of secondary evidence rather than the best evidence? Give some examples of secondary evidence. (§13.7)

10. What are the provisions of Federal Rule 1003? How does this differ from traditional state rules? Has this provision been adopted by any states? What is a "duplicate?" (§13.7)

11. What is the rationale for authorizing the use of summaries of material in documents rather than the documents themselves? What is meant by laying a proper foundation for the use of summaries? (§13.8)

12. What is the basis for the rule that generally excludes medical and other scientific treatises as independent evidence of the theories and opinions expressed therein? Have any states adopted a contrary view? (§13.9)

13. In the case of *United States v. Dockins,* the government attempted to link the defendant to a previous conviction by introducing a fingerprint card reflecting the arrest of the defendant in another city. On appeal, the defendant claimed that the document had not been properly authenticated because the agent who testified had no knowledge, other than from reading the document, that the fingerprint card actually came from the police department. Was the fingerprint card self-authenticating under Federal Rule 901? Was it an abuse of discretion to admit the document? Was the fingerprint card properly authenticated? (*United States v. Dockins*, Part II)

14. In *McKeehan v. Florida,* defendant McKeehan was found guilty of robbery with a firearm, grand theft, aggravated assault with a firearm, and kidnapping with intent to commit a felony. All of these crimes were allegedly committed at a Sleep Inn Motel in Orlando. An officer was permitted to orally identify the defendant from a security video at a different motel from where the crimes occurred. The video from the other motel was not shown. On appeal, McKeehan asserted that the trial court committed error in violating the best evidence rule by allowing the state to use oral testimony to prove the contents of a videotape (a writing), rather than with the tape itself. Did the appellate court affirm or reverse based on the admission of the officer's statements? Did this practice violate the best evidence rule? Why or why not? Would the harmless error rule help the government? (*McKeehan v. Florida*, Part II)

15. In the case of *Colorado v. Huehn,* the government prosecuted the defendant for illegally accessing an ATM that he had earlier properly been allowed to service as part of his usual job activities. As part of the prosecution, the court allowed the introduction of computer-generated data that tended to demonstrate at what times the ATM safe had been opened. Defendant Huehn contended that the trial court abused its discretion in admitting into evidence computer-generated records that were not sufficiently authenticated. Four of the documentary exhibits were records generated for the bank by a service company from computer-generated records. Did the reviewing court think that the computer-generated records could be admitted under the business records exception to the hearsay rule? Are these types of documents easily altered or faked? Could they be faked with effort? Should the originals be produced? What would constitute the original, because it came from a computer? Did the appellate court reverse the conviction for theft from the ATM? (*Colorado v. Huehn*, Part II)

Chapter 14
Real Evidence

Objectives

Real evidence is evidence that is addressed directly to the senses such as by sight, hearing, or taste. Real evidence has often been referred to by the terms "demonstrative" or "physical" evidence. Because of its nature, real evidence may prove to be more persuasive than oral or documentary evidence and oral testimony, but it still must pass several admissibility tests. Some of these tests are unique to real evidence and the evidence must still pass the usual hurdles of relevancy, materiality, and competency. The purpose of this chapter is to examine the general rules concerning the admissibility of real evidence and to indicate the specific rules that relate to various types of real evidence, such as photographs, recordings, diagrams, and maps.

The objectives of this chapter are to:

1. Define *real evidence* and distinguish real evidence from documentary evidence and oral testimony.

2. Emphasize the importance of the use of real evidence in assisting the court and jury in reaching a conclusion.

3. List the admissibility requirements relating to real evidence and review the cases that interpret the *chain of custody* rule.

4. Give examples of situations in which the person of the witness may be displayed to the jury to show injury or other evidence.

5. Explain the admissibility rules relating to the introduction of articles connected with the crime: for example, clothing found at the scene, bloodstains, paint chips, dust on clothing, and debris.

6. Interpret the decisions that allow the jury to view the scene of the crime.

7. List and discuss the rules relating to the preparation and introduction of photographs in evidence.

8. Present cases concerning the admissibility of motion pictures and list the steps followed in laying a foundation for the admission of motion picture evidence.

9. Discuss the difference between X-ray and photograph admissibility requirements.

10. List the conditions for admitting sound recordings into evidence and highlight the dangers of relying on this type of evidence.

11. Discuss the duty of the police and prosecutor to preserve and disclose evidence that is favorable to the defense.

Discussion Outline

§14.1   Introduction
       A.   Definition of Real Evidence
       B.   Examples of Real Evidence

§14.2   Admissibility Requirements
       A.   Establishment of a Chain or Continuity of Custody
       B.   Necessity
       C.   Relationship to Crime
       D.   Proper Identification

§14.3   Exhibition of Person

§14.4   Articles Connected with the Crime
       A.   Weapons
       B.   Instruments Used in the Crime
       C.   Clothing
       D.   Bloodstains
       E.   Narcotics and Narcotics Paraphernalia
       F.   Other Types of Evidence

§14.5   View of the Scene
       A.   Purpose of Viewing the Scene
       B.   Procedure followed in Viewing the Scene

§14.6   Photographs
       A.   Posed Photographs
       B.   Gruesome Photographs
       C.   Time of Taking
       D.   Color Photographs
       E.   Enlargements and Aerial Photographs

§14.7   Motion Pictures and Videotapes

§14.8   X-rays

§14.9   Sound Recordings
    A. Laying the Foundation
    B. Admissibility Tests

§14.10   Diagrams, Maps, and Models

§14.11   Courtroom Demonstrations and Experiments

§14.12   Preservation and Disclosure of Evidence Favorable to the Defense
    A. Extent of the Constitutional Duty to Disclose Exculpatory Evidence
    B. Results of Failure to Comply with Constitutional Mandates

§14.13   Summary

Review Questions

1. What is real evidence? Distinguish it from documentary evidence and oral testimony. (§14.1)

2. List four general rules regarding the admissibility of real evidence. How does the party offering real evidence authenticate the item? (§14.2)

3. What is meant by the term *chain of custody*? Is real evidence admitted if there is a break in the chain of custody? Explain. (§14.2)

4. What factors are considered in determining whether real evidence is connected with a crime? Give some examples. (§14.2)

5. What are the factors that the judge considers in determining whether the exhibition of the person of the victim is to be allowed? (§14.3)

6. May a weapon such as a gun, allegedly used in the commission of a crime, be introduced in evidence? Are there any conditions on its admission? If so, what are they? Must the party offering the weapon establish an absolute chain of custody? (§14.4)

7. What is the general rule concerning the admissibility of clothing, such as that worn by the accused at the time of the crime? Give other examples of evidence that is admissible as an article or instrument connected with a crime. What are the requirements for admitting narcotics, narcotics paraphernalia, and records? (§14.4)

8. Does a judge have the authority in a criminal case to permit the jurors to view the premises where the crime was alleged to have been committed? What is the procedure for viewing the premises, if it is authorized? Is it error for a judge to refuse to allow the jury to be present at the scene of the crime? (§14.5)

9. What are the requirements for the admissibility of photographs? Are photographs admissible if the officer who takes the photographs violates the Constitution when taking the photographs? Explain. (§14.6)

10. What is the rationale for not allowing the admission of gruesome photographs? What factors are considered when determining admissibility? (§14.6)

11. What evidence is required in laying the foundation for the admissibility of motion pictures at trial? Give some examples of the use of motion pictures in criminal cases. What are the requirements for the admissibility of videotapes? Explain. Does the fact that parts of the tape are inaudible require exclusion? (§14.7)

12. Are sound recordings admissible in evidence? If so, what are the requirements? What are the dangers of using sound recordings in evidence? (§14.9)

13. What are the requirements for laying a foundation for the admission of sound recordings? (§14.9)

14. May diagrams, maps, models, and blackboard drawings be used to explain testimony during a trial? If so, are there any conditions on their use? (§14.10)

15. Does the law require the prosecution to turn over exculpatory evidence to the defendant? If the prosecution is required to turn over exculpatory evidence to the defendant, what are the consequences for failing to do so? (§14.12)

16. In *Schmerber v. California*, blood to be used in a blood-alcohol test was taken from a driver who had been arrested for driving under the influence. Under what provisions of the Constitution was the taking of the blood challenged? What was the decision of the court concerning the use of blood for this purpose? (*Schmerber v. California*, Part II)

17. In the case of *Illinois v. Cowans*, the defendant was found guilty of one count of possession of a controlled substance with intent to deliver. On appeal, the defendant challenged the sufficiency of the evidence and contended that the stipulated facts, together with the entire trial record, failed to establish a complete chain of custody for the real evidence, the controlled substance. Before real evidence may be admitted at trial, the prosecution must provide an adequate foundation either by way of live testimony or a stipulation that establishes that the item sought to be introduced is the actual item involved in the alleged offense and that its condition is substantially unchanged since it was seized. The state seized some containers near here defendant had been standing and sent them to the state lab for processing. The lab processed some containers containing rock cocaine. Did the officers properly contain the evidence? What must they do to prove the evidence tested came from the defendant? Did they keep a proper chain of custody sufficient to authenticate the evidence as having come from defendant? Why or why not? Would you have upheld his conviction? (*Illinois v. Cowans*, Part II)

18. In the case of *Underwood v. State*, the defendant was indicted for capital murder. The indictment charged that the defendant murdered the victim by shooting her with a pistol during the course of a kidnapping. The jury returned a verdict of guilty and found that the defendant should be sentenced to death. On appeal, the defendant argued that the introduction of the videotape of the crime scene depicting the victim's body outweighed the tape's probative value and the introduction of numerous gruesome photographs outweighed their probative value. What were the comments of the court concerning the general rule relating to the admissibility of gruesome photographs? What factors must the judge consider when deciding on the admissibility of gruesome photographs? Do the same standards apply to determining admissibility of videotapes? Were the videotapes and the photographs properly admitted by the trial court in this case? (*Underwood v. State*, Part II)

Chapter 15
Results of Examinations and Tests

Objectives

Evidence collected at a crime scene or otherwise related to a criminal prosecution may be tested and returned for use in court while some real evidence may be destroyed during testing and be rendered inadmissible. In any event, evidence derived from the testing or inspection of real evidence may be admissible if it meets a variety of tests for relevancy, materiality, competency, and chain of custody, among the other requirements that apply to specific types of scientific tests.

This chapter examines the general and specific rules relating to examinations and discusses the substance of the tests. Requirements concerning intoxication tests, blood grouping tests, polygraph examinations, fingerprint comparisons, ballistics experiments, speed detection readings, voice identification, neutron activation analysis, and DNA tests are analyzed.

The objectives of this chapter are to:

1. State and explain the conditions surrounding the use of evidence from the person, such as blood, clothing, marks and bruises, and saliva samples. Emphasize the impact of scientific tests in criminal cases. Indicate the factors considered in assessing the reliability of scientific tests.

2. Enumerate the special rules relating to the admissibility and weight of intoxication tests. This includes blood tests, breath tests, horizontal gaze nystagmus tests, and urine tests. Discuss implied consent statutes.

3. Discuss the requirements relating to blood grouping tests and rules concerning admissibility of the results in court.

4. Generally explain the theory of the polygraph examination and the requirements for use of the results in a criminal case. Point out the three conflicting approaches to the use of polygraph evidence and review decisions concerning the admissibility of polygraph evidence.

5. Distinguish between polygraph and truth serum procedures, in method and admissibility of results.

6. Briefly relate the purpose of taking fingerprints and clarify the rules concerning the admissibility of fingerprint evidence in a criminal case. Explain the requirements placed on police officers when taking fingerprints.

7. After referring to past discussions of ballistics, interpret the rules relating to the use of experts who testify about ballistics experiments.

8. Briefly consider the RADAR (Radio Detection And Ranging) principle and clarify the restrictions on the use of evidence obtained by this method.

9. Understand the practice and requirements for admissibility of laser devices for calculating vehicle speed.

10. Trace the development of the spectrogram voice identification process and the limited admissibility of such evidence in recent years.

11. Describe the neutron activation analysis process and explain the rules relating to the admissibility of the results of such analysis.

12. Describe deoxyribonucleic acid (DNA) testing, and the admissibility requirements for this type of evidence.

Discussion Outline

§15.1   Introduction
    A. Importance of Scientific Evidence
    B. Tests for Admission

§15.2   Examination of the Person

§15.3   Intoxication Tests
    A. Blood Tests
    B. Breath Tests
    C. Urine Tests
    D. Horizontal Gaze Nystagmus Tests
    E. Implied Consent Statutes

§15.4   Blood Grouping Tests and Blood Comparisons

§15.5   Polygraph Examinations
    A. Polygraphy Theory
    B. Three Approaches to Admissibility
    C. Tests for Admission

§15.6   "Truth Serum" Results

§15.7   Fingerprint Comparisons

§15.8   Ballistics Experiments
    A. Identifying Specific Firearms
    B. Source of Ammunition
    C. Powder Patterns

§15.9   Speed Detection Readings
    A. RADAR (Radio Detection and Ranging) Devices
    B. VASCAR (Visual Average Speed Computer and Record) Units
    C. Laser Speed Detection Devices

§15.10   Voice Identification
    A. Spectrogram
    B. Computer-Assisted Voice Identification Systems
    C. Limitations of Use

§15.11   Neutron Activation Analysis
    A. Theoretical Basis
    B. Proof of Use of Firearm
    C. Limitations

§15.12   Deoxyribonucleic Acid (DNA) Tests
    A. Scientific Principle
    B. Reliability
    C. Admissibility

§15.13   Other Examinations and Tests

§15.14   Summary

Review Questions

1. May testimony concerning the results of experiments and tests made out of court be admitted in a criminal trial? What are the requirements? What are the considerations in determining the admissibility of evidence under the Federal Rules of Evidence?

2. What was the decision in the *Daubert* case? How did *Daubert* change prior practice in federal courts? (§15.1)

3. What constitutional provisions are usually referred to when challenging examinations of the body for such things as traces of blood, bruises, and marks? (§15.2)

4. In addition to blood, what other substances are used to determine blood-alcohol content? What other tests are performed and what conditions must be met before using this evidence in court? (§15.3)

5. What is the purpose of implied consent statutes? Have these been held unconstitutional? May evidence of refusal to take a blood-alcohol test be introduced at trial? Explain. (§15.3)

6. Give examples of the uses of blood grouping tests and blood comparisons in criminal cases. (§15.4)

7. State in nontechnical terms how the polygraph operates. What three approaches have been taken by various courts to determine the admissibility of polygraph evidence? Is polygraph evidence per se inadmissible? (§15.5)

8. How does the "truth serum" procedure differ from the polygraph test? Is evidence obtained while a person is under the influence of "truth serum" admissible in a criminal case? Explain. (§15.6)

9. Is testimony regarding fingerprint comparisons for identification purposes authorized in a criminal case? How can one qualify as a fingerprint expert? Are the police required to take fingerprints at the scene of a crime? Must the officer give the *Miranda* warnings before taking fingerprints? (§15.7)

10. How does one qualify as a witness to testify about the results of ballistics experiments? Give examples of some of the subjects of ballistics expert testimony. (§15.8)

11. How is RADAR used to measure speed? What are the requirements for using the results in court? (§15.9)

12. What is the principle behind laser speed detection? How has the admissibility of this evidence been facilitated by some state legislatures? (§15.9)

13. What is the theory of the spectrogram voice identification technique? Are the results of this technique admissible in a criminal case for identification purposes? (§15.10)

14. Has any court approved the use of neutron activation analysis as a means of detecting the presence of certain chemical elements? Are there any dangers in using this method? Explain. (§15.11)

15. Describe the deoxyribonucleic acid (DNA) test. How is this test used in criminal cases? Has the test been approved by state courts? By federal courts? Do the courts take judicial notice of the reliability of DNA evidence? List and discuss the defendant's avenues of attack. (§15.12)

16. The defendant in the case of *United States v. Martinez* was convicted of sexual abuse of a minor. On appeal, he challenged the use of DNA profiling evidence by the trial court. After referring to other cases and publications, the court reached some conclusions. What is the test for assessing the reliability of novel scientific evidence? How does the *Frye* test differ from the Federal Rules of Evidence (*Daubert*) test? Did the court find that DNA profiling meets admissibility requirements? If the general theory of DNA testing is valid, how can the defense challenge the use of such evidence? (*United States v. Martinez*, Part II)

17. In this federal case, the defendant was convicted of submitting false claims to Medicare and Medicaid, obstructing justice, and making false declarations to a grand jury. The sole issue on appeal was whether the district court erred when it excluded evidence of a polygraph examination offered by the defendant. The reviewing court discussed the various methods of conducting polygraph examinations and reviewed the decisions handed down by the United States Supreme Court, as well as decisions rendered by the circuit court. According to the decision in this and other cases, are the results of polygraph examinations inadmissible per se in federal court? Under what circumstances, if any, may polygraph evidence be admitted? If polygraph evidence is admitted to corroborate or impeach the testimony of a witness at trial, may the trial court exclude the polygraph evidence on other grounds? Did the district court abuse its discretion in excluding the polygraph evidence in this case? (*United States v. Gilliard*, Part II)

18. In the *City of Cleveland Heights v. Katz*, a police officer observed a vehicle traveling at an elevated level of speed and clocked the vehicle with a radar unit. A municipal court convicted Katz of speeding and he appealed, contending that the radar gun and the instruments used to calibrate the radar gun had not been shown to have been properly tested. What steps must a police officer take to accurately clock a potential speeder with scientific instruments? What steps can a police department be forced to follow in order to prove that an instrument worked properly? Was the radar device properly maintained and serviced? Would you have overturned the conviction? Why or why not? (*City of Cleveland Heights v. Katz*, Part II)

Chapter 16
Evidence Unconstitutionally Obtained

Objectives

Unconstitutionally seized evidence is generally not admissible for positive proof of guilt, but it may be useful for other purposes, such as impeachment. Therefore, evidence may possess relevancy, materiality and be crucially important to the criminal prosecution of a case, but if it has been obtained illegally, it may be excluded for proof of guilt. The purpose of the material in this chapter is first to impress upon the reader the necessity of following the Constitution and the rules established by the Supreme Court in obtaining evidence, and second, to state the rules relating to the kinds of evidence that are most often excluded due to the illegality under which the evidence has been collected.

The objectives of this chapter are to:

1. Emphasize the rationale for excluding relevant evidence that is obtained in violation of the Constitution.

2. State and trace the history of the exclusionary rule as it relates to search and seizure.

3. State the approved methods of obtaining evidence without violating search and seizure rules.

4. Review legislation that prohibits interception of communications under some conditions but allows interception under other conditions.

5. State and explain the rules relating to the admissibility of confessions and the requirements that must be met if a confession is to be admitted in evidence in a criminal case.

6. Develop an understanding of the self-incrimination rule as it relates to the admissibility of evidence and the limits on the application of this rule.

7. Identify the due process clauses of the Constitution, define due process, and relate how these provisions determine the competency of certain types of evidence.

8. Referring to case decisions, summarize the rules relating to the right to counsel and explain how failure to grant this right will in some instances make evidence inadmissible.

Discussion Outline

§16.1   Introduction
    A. Rationale for Excluding Unconstitutionally Obtained Evidence
    B. Provisions of the Bill of Rights Most Often Used to Challenge the Use of Evidence

§16.2   Development of the Exclusionary Rule
    A. Statement of the English Rule
    B. Development of the Rule in the United States
    C. Application to the States (*Mapp v. Ohio*)

§16.3   Search and Seizure Exclusions
    A. Provisions of the Constitution Relating to Search and Seizure
    B. Application of the Exclusionary Rule (*Mapp v. Ohio*)
    C. Modification of the Exclusionary Rule (*United States v. Leon*)
    D. Exceptions to the Warrant Rule
        1. Search incident to a Lawful Arrest
        2. Search after a Waiver of Constitutional Rights
        3. Search of a Vehicle That is Moving or About to Be Moved
        4. Seizure of Evidence When No Search Is Required (Plain View)
        5. Seizure of Evidence From Premises Not Protected by the Fourth Amendment (Open Fields)
        6. Search by a Private Individual
        7. Search After Lawful Impoundment
        8. Stop-and-Frisk Search

§16.4   Exclusion of Evidence Obtained by Illegal Wiretapping or Eavesdropping
    A. Pertinent Supreme Court Decisions Relating to Wiretapping and Eavesdropping
    B. Title 18 United States Code §§ 3121-3126
    C. Electronic Monitoring and Recording

§16.5   Exclusion of Confessions Obtained in Violation of Constitutional Provisions
    A. The Free and Voluntary Rule
    B. The Delay in Arraignment Rule
    C. The *Miranda* Rule
    D. Public Safety Exception
    E. The Effect of Legislation on the Admissibility of Confessions

§16.6   Self-Incrimination and Related Protections
    A. Provision of the Constitution Relating to Self-Incrimination
    B. *Schmerber v. California*
    C. *Brooks v. Tennessee*

§16.7   Due Process Exclusions
    A. Provisions of the Constitution Relating to Due Process
    B. Examples of Procedures That Violate Due Process

§16.8   Right to Counsel as It Relates to the Exclusion of Evidence
    A. Provision of the Constitution Guaranteeing the Right to Counsel
    B. *Escobedo v. Illinois* and *Miranda v. Arizona*
    C. *Edwards v. Arizona, Michigan v. Harvey,* and *Michigan v. Jackson*
    D. Right to Counsel at the Lineup or Other Confrontation for Identification

§16.9   Summary

Review Questions

1. What is the rationale for not admitting evidence that is obtained in violation of the Constitution? (§16.1)

2. What are the provisions of the Fourth, Fifth, and Sixth Amendments that limit the use of evidence in criminal cases? (§16.1 and Bill of Rights)

3. Define the *exclusionary rule.* What is its purpose? How has the rule been modified in recent years? What is the "derivative evidence" rule? What is the *good faith* exception? (§16.2)

4. How does the rule relating to the use of illegally seized evidence in England differ from that in the United States? Which rule do you feel has the most merit? Discuss. (§16.2)

5. State at least five ways of making legal searches without warrants and give the rationale for each exception. (§16.3)

6. What is the justification for seizing evidence from a person incident to a lawful arrest? State and explain the *Chimel* rule. (§16.3)

7. In the case of *United States v. Thornton,* what conduct did the officer perform that made the arrest and search incident to arrest illegal? (§16.3)

8. In 1984, the United States Supreme Court carved out a limited exception to the exclusionary rule known as the public safety exception. Define the exception stated in that case and the rationale of the Court in authorizing the exception. What are the requirements for a valid search warrant? (§16.3)

9. May the protection of the Fourth Amendment be waived? If so, what are the requirements? Who has the burden of proving waiver? (§16.3)

10. Define the moving vehicle exception. Does the moving vehicle exception apply to a motor home? Explain. (§16.3)

11. What is the open fields exception? What factors are to be considered in determining whether property is a part of the curtilage? Does the Fourth Amendment apply to searches by private individuals? (§16.3)

12. What is the rationale for authorizing the seizure of objects from an impounded car? Define *plain view* as an exception to the warrant requirement. (§16.3)

13. Do the provisions of the Fourth Amendment apply when evidence is obtained by wiretapping and eavesdropping? Is the seizure of evidence by the use of an illegal wiretap or eavesdropping permitted? Are there any exceptions to the rule that an order must be obtained before wiretap evidence is admissible? (§16.4)

14. Why is a confession inadmissible if it is not freely and voluntarily given? Define *free and voluntary* and give case examples. (§16.5)

15. What degree of proof is required of the prosecution to show that a confession is voluntary? Discuss. What factors are considered? (§16.5)

16. What is the *delay in arraignment* rule as it relates to confessions? In relation to this, give the facts and holding of the *Mallory* case. (§16.5)

17. What are the four warnings required by the United States Supreme Court as stated in *Miranda v. Arizona*? At what stage are the warnings required? (§16.5)

18. If the *Miranda* warnings are not given, is evidence from the confession excluded for all purposes? Discuss. (§16.5)

19. What are the provisions of the Omnibus Crime Control Act relating to the admissibility of confessions? (§16.5)

20. What is the provision of the Constitution that relates to self-incrimination? Are nontestimonial communications protected by this constitutional provision? Discuss. (§16.6)

21. There are two provisions of the Constitution that include the phrase "due process of law." What are they? Give an example of a situation in which the due process clause of the Fourteenth Amendment was violated. (§16.7)

22. What provisions of the Bill of Rights protect a person's right to counsel in criminal cases? At what point in the judicial process does the right to counsel attach? If a confession is obtained after counsel is requested by the accused, is it admissible evidence? (§16.8)

23. State the rule relating to the right to have counsel present at a lineup or other confrontation for identification. (§16.8)

24. In the case of *United States v. Leon*, a judge, after evaluating all of the evidence, issued a facially valid search warrant. Police officers, acting in good faith, executed the warrant and found large quantities of drugs. The warrant was later determined to be invalid due to insufficient probable cause. What was the opinion of the United States Supreme Court concerning the admissibility of the evidence obtained by the officers? What was the rationale of the court in reaching its conclusion? What was the rule established in that case? (*United States v. Leon*, Part II)

25. In the case of *United States v. Thornton*, a police officer observed the defendant driving a vehicle that would not pull all the way up to where the unmarked police vehicle was located and would not pass the police vehicle. The officer checked the license plate and determined that it was not registered to the car he was observing. When the driver was pulled over, he became very nervous and distracted. As the officer patted down the man for weapons, he asked him if he had any illegal drugs and the man pulled out some marijuana. At this point the officer arrested Thornton and searched his car incident to arrest, discovering more incriminating evidence. After his conviction Thornton appealed the alleged illegal stop and search of his person and of the vehicle. Should the court overturn his conviction because the arrest was illegal under the Fourth Amendment? Was the search of the vehicle illegal? Was the pat down of his person consistent with *Miranda v. Arizona*? *(United States v. Thornton*, Part II)

26. The defendant in the case of *United States v. Edmo* was convicted of unlawfully possessing a firearm while using a controlled substance. He appealed the denial of his motions to suppress the results of a urine test and an incriminating statement made after police officers requested a urine sample. The defendant contends that, in requiring him to submit to a urine test, the police violated his Fourth Amendment right against unreasonable searches, his Fifth Amendment right against self-incrimination, and his Sixth Amendment right to counsel. Did the police requiring the defendant to submit to a urine test violate the Fourth Amendment right against unreasonable search and seizures, the Fifth Amendment right against self-incrimination, or the Sixth Amendment right to counsel? Give reasons for your answers. (*United States v. Edmo*, Part II)

27. In the case of *Horton v. California,* a police officer prepared an affidavit for a search warrant, which referred to the proceeds of a robbery and weapons. The warrant issued by the magistrate only authorized a search for the proceeds. While executing the search warrant the officer seized weapons in plain view. Was the seizure of the weapons justified under the warrant? What was the U.S. Supreme Court's decision concerning the requirement that the discovery of evidence in plain view be "inadvertent?" What are the two conditions that must be satisfied in order for a plain view seizure to be valid? (*Horton v. California*, §16.3)

28. The defendant in the case of *United States v. Reno* was convicted of various drug offenses. The arresting officer noticed that the defendant threw some trash in a dumpster and later took a look at the trash, which revealed drug manufacturing material. The trash contained seven used syringes, 91 empty pseudoephedrine "blister packs," and three empty pseudoephedrine pill bottles. The officer imme-

diately recognized the pseudoephedrine-related items as those commonly used in the manufacture of methamphetamine, and the syringes as drug paraphernalia. The officer followed the defendant to his home, where the defendant was arrested while standing next to his truck. Subsequent to the arrest, the police, without a warrant, searched Reno's truck, discovering more incriminating material. Should the police have arrested the defendant after observing him throw drug manufacturing materials in the dumpster? Was probable cause shown? Was the search of his truck incident to arrest proper? What did the *Reno* Court say? (*United States v. Reno*, Part II)